ADRIAN NEWEY

AN ILLUSTRATED BIOGRAPHY OF F1'S GREATEST DESIGNER

ADRIAN NEWEY

AN ILLUSTRATED BIOGRAPHY OF F1'S GREATEST DESIGNER

Frank Hopkinson

IVY PRESS

Quarto

First published in 2026 by Ivy Press,
an imprint of The Quarto Group.
One Triptych Place,
London, SE1 9SH,
United Kingdom
T (0)20 7700 9000
www.Quarto.com

EEA Representation, WTS Tax d.o.o.,
Žanova ulica 3, 4000 Kranj, Slovenia
www.wts-tax.si

A catalogue record for this book is available from the British Library.

ISBN 978-1-83600-891-0
Ebook ISBN 978-1-83600-892-7

10 9 8 7 6 5 4 3 2 1

Cover and design by Cara Rogers
Publisher Richard Green
Editor Frank Hopkinson
Editorial Assistant Nayima Ali
Senior Designer Renata Latipova
Senior Production Manager Alex Merrett

Printed in Guangdong, China TT122025

Adrian Newey – An Illustrated Biography of F1's Greatest Designer is an independent publication, both unauthorised and unofficial.

CONTENTS

INTRODUCTION

Adrian Newey was once asked if he could see air. It was a claim promoted by his former Red Bull boss Christian Horner, though in a light-hearted vein. 'No, of course not,' was the immediate reply, answered with scientific rigour. But then he thought about it some more. 'I can picture it,' Newey said, gazing into the middle distance. 'And if I try to be objective, that's perhaps one of my strengths – that I can actually picture things well in my mind's eye.'

RIGHT: Adrian Newey's Aston Martin Valkyrie in its Le Mans spec. Aston Martin put a limited number of ten on sale in 2025 for £5m.

He was talking about airflow. Many years spent with strands of wool attached to 1:25 and 1:40 scale models in wind tunnels located across the UK from Southampton to Kensington to Bicester and beyond have given him an uncanny ability to assess the effects of aerodynamic surfaces on drag and downforce.

Enzo Ferrari famously said that aerodynamics was for people who could not build engines, but over the last forty years it has been the biggest performance differentiator between F1 cars. The arrival of the Mercedes hybrid engine in 2014 might have put a small dent in that theory, but the success of McLaren in winning the constructors' title in 2024 and 2025 with a customer Mercedes engine has shown that a team needs more than sheer bhp.

Classifying Adrian Newey as the world's most influential motorsport aerodynamicist is only telling a fraction of the story. Although his degree from Southampton University was in aeronautical engineering, his childhood passion for building cars gave him an important insight into the mechanical engineering side of racing cars.

When he joined March Engineering in Bicester – one of the principal chassis suppliers for the North American IndyCar and sports cars series – he was able to combine his work as a designer with race-engineering; for Johnny Cecotto, Bobby Rahal and Michael Andretti, before moving on to Newman-Haas and race-engineering Mario Andretti for a sky-high salary of $400,000 (in 1987). He had already proven his worth by designing the Indy 500-winning March 85C and the March 86C – his redesigned March sports car won the Daytona 24 Hours.

The ability to listen to drivers' feedback and make adjustments to the car in response is one of Adrian's strongest suits. It's a quality acknowledged by former

World Champion Alain Prost, who he helped win his fourth drivers' title in 1993. 'I loved talking to Adrian. Adrian is listening to you, asking questions all the time. You never have an argument with Adrian,' recalled the driver nicknamed 'The Professor'. 'And it's fantastic for the engineers working with him, it brings energy and synergy in terms of the brain, that capacity is fantastic.'

ABOVE: Newey steered Red Bull to eight drivers' titles and six constructors' championships.

Another aspect unique among designers is his experience of driving performance cars. Unlike many of his contemporaries Adrian has competed at Le Mans, both historic and current, and owns a classic Lotus 49B which he has driven around the streets of Monaco, no easy task with a gear lever ensuring one-handed steering for a large proportion of the lap. This has only helped in his diagnosis of turn-in understeer and all the remedies that can be applied to dial it out.

He has won drivers' and constructors' championships with Williams, McLaren and Red Bull that have made him the most successful F1 designer of all time, but perhaps his greatest triumph came when the technical regulations were at their most restrictive. The re-set of the rules for 2022 were aimed at allowing cars to follow each other more closely and provide the overtaking action that had been lacking in earlier seasons. To enable this, designers were allowed to produce ground effect cars, with sculpted Venturi tunnels that effectively gained downforce by sucking cars to the asphalt.

Newey was the only current designer who had worked with ground effect cars before they were banished in the early 1980s. He was well aware of the dangers of 'porpoising' – when that suction suddenly lets go – and though his RB18 lagged behind the Ferrari at first, that was merely a hangover from the 2021 season-long battle with Mercedes. Once the team could reduce the weight of the car, the evolution into the RB19 produced a 2023 season total of 21 wins out of 22 – the record books rewritten.

It is this unique skillset that Newey has taken to Aston Martin. The Formula 1 paddock waits to see if he can interpret the 2026 rules re-set and produce yet another race-winning car. His move away from a near-20-year residency at Red Bull took many by surprise, but the team he moved to fulfilled all the qualities of teams he has joined in the past. Leyton House was the first rung on the ladder and a lesson learned in working for a team on the verge of insolvency. Both Williams and McLaren had enjoyed success in the past but had dropped back and needed direction. Similarly the fledgling Red Bull team needed Newey's engineering excellence and organisational sense, and like Williams and McLaren, had the finance to deliver car upgrades at a speed to match their chief designer's inventiveness.

Aston Martin, with Lawrence Stroll in charge, has the ambition and the money to deliver a World Championship. When asked at a press conference why he had joined Aston Martin, Adrian's reply was a single word: 'Lawrence'. Newey likes the old school approach of working for a single decision-maker, not a corporate structure – which Red Bull has become after the death of Dietrich Mateschitz – or the 'matrix' form of management he couldn't abide at McLaren.

Yet despite his fearsome reputation as a title winner, workaholic and 'the most competitive man in F1' it would be a mistake to think of Adrian Newey as a boring technocrat wrapped up in a world of computational fluid dynamics. Like Jeremy Clarkson he was expelled from Repton public school, but for far more reckless behaviour than *The Grand Tour* presenter. This is a man who has driven a scooter into Monaco harbour (intentionally), crashed a motorbike into a paddock restaurant at the French Grand Prix (accidentally) and had his fair share of off-track excursions in his own racing career. Not to mention many escapades with 'terrible influence' David Coulthard.

In motorsport there is the drivers' Triple Crown – a win at Le Mans, the Indy 500 and the Monaco Grand Prix. As a designer, Adrian has won multiple Monaco GPs, multiple Indy 500s, but has yet to create a car that has won Le Mans. Having produced the Aston Martin Valkyrie and the ambitious £5m hypercar, the Red Bull RB 17, it is clearly within his skillset to become the designer equivalent of Graham Hill, the only driver to have won all three. Whether he still has the hours left remains to be seen. He has already given the world enough racing machinery to make his position as the world's greatest motorsport designer unbeatable. And the next five years may well add to what is already an overflowing trophy cupboard. As Sir Jackie Stewart has said: 'We have had many great drivers in Formula 1, but even fewer who can impact a team as much as Adrian Newey.'

1

HILL
SHELL

CAR FANATIC

Adrian came into this world on Boxing Day 1958, while his parents were driving around Colchester accompanied by a midwife. His mother's waters broke and they had to make a dash to the nearest house. Adrian was born in a random house amid the kindness of strangers.

Father Richard ran a veterinary practice in Stratford-upon-Avon, which included a larger, farm animal practice. Vivacious and artistic mother Edwina had been an ambulance driver in the war and had met Adrian's father when she brought her Pyrenean mountain dog to his surgery.

Edwina had a son from a previous marriage, Tim, who was sent off to board at Repton School. There was a significant age gap between Adrian and his step-brother. F1's official interviewer, Tom Clarkson, once asked Adrian if his famed competitiveness was down to sibling rivalry.

'My brother's seven years older than me, so as an age gap it's too different to be competitive with each other,' he replied. 'It's a question I ask myself and the truth is, I'm not exactly sure, but I think part of it was when I was at school, I always thought about things a bit differently. One example that's always stuck in my head is that when I was about 12 or so, we had a lesson in science on friction, and it was actually a video that went through what friction does, how it works, etc.

'At the end of it, the teacher said, "So everybody, is friction a good thing?" I was the only one who stuck up my hand and said, "Well, without friction we'd all fall over. I wouldn't be able to stand up because we'd just slide around everywhere," and everybody laughed and the teacher laughed at me. It's a silly little example, but it made me feel as if I needed to prove myself. The feeling of needing to prove yourself is, in truth, probably a close cousin to being competitive.'

Adrian had to endure some terrible rows between his parents as a child – both had incendiary tendencies, which

PREVIOUS PAGE: 'King of Monaco' Graham Hill in the Lotus 49B in 1969, just before the high-rise rear wings were banned.

BELOW: Adrian's family business helped keep the British Empire neat and well presented.

may well be one of the reasons he shies away from confrontation or hostile negotiations. His second wife, Marigold, took a part in his negotiations with both McLaren and Red Bull – not unlike the Mark Webber/Ann Neal, driver/manager relationship – while his move from Red Bull to Aston Martin would be brokered by the wily Eddie Jordan.

Rows at home could be exacerbated by Edwina's love of a drink or two, something that didn't go unnoticed by the family's African grey parrot, who would mimic the sound of her preprandial drink sessions, imitating all the sounds of the pouring of a sweet Martini.

His father's family had run a manufacturing business in Birmingham, producing hooks, eyes and fasteners from 1798, a time when Birmingham was the workshop of the British Empire – a scenario not unlike those portrayed as the background to *Peaky Blinders*. In the 1960s, the managing director of the company, which had premises in Summer Lane and a three-storey factory on Brearley Street, was Mr Martin Newey – so it's perhaps no coincidence that Adrian's full name is Adrian Martin Newey.

The family heritage in engineering from this business allowed Richard Newey to buy cars – Lotus Elans and Mini Coopers – and tinker with them for hours on end. Adrian describes him in his autobiography as having 'mad but ingenious ideas' and that he liked nothing better than a challenge: 'How can I do this differently? How can I do this better?'

He also had an extraordinary eye for detail and the penalty for carrying too much weight. In this instance it was not weight in a car, but weight in the Newey family rucksack carried on all camping trips. The need to make things lighter, an eye for detail, a love of mechanical engineering and a propensity to think outside the box are all characteristics that Adrian has inherited and employed with phenomenal success through his career.

He described his father as Caractacus Potts, the madcap inventor from *Chitty Chitty Bang Bang*, and his attractive mother as an artistic maverick – and the combination of both qualities has led to a lifetime of standing at a drawing board finessing the fine details of the world's most expensive racing machinery.

LOTUS 49B
FORD F-I
1:12
BIG SCALE 4
ゴールドリーフロータス
TAMIYA

At four he went to a local convent school where the nuns tried to cure him of his left-handedness. As with Leonardo da Vinci, their work was in vain. Leonardo is described by the Getty Museum as 'one of the greatest draftsmen in history, and his sinistral handedness left a little-known trace in his drawings: the slope of his lines.' When da Vinci shaded in areas of his sketches, he drew hatching lines from top left to bottom right. As does Adrian.

After the convent he was shipped off to Emscote Lawn prep school in Warwick, which took both day-boys and boarders. Adrian was caned for pranks more than once. It was the kind of English public school where a Mr Randle, the music teacher, might punish a child (not Adrian) by making them keep a matchbox in their mouth for a whole lesson. Pupils could face a whack across the buttocks with a hockey stick for misbehaviour. Revelations shared on the now-closed Emscote Lawn school Facebook page give an eye-opening insight into the practices of public school education.

ABOVE AND TOP LEFT: Two large-scale kits from Tamiya that helped give the young designer a grasp of F1 racing machinery and its component parts.

LEFT: Unlike most teenage kit builders Adrian went on to buy his very own Lotus 49B and race it on the streets of Monaco in the historic F1 races.

J.H. Riley the headmaster was a stern, uncompromising figure who railed against Adrian's 'silliness' in his final school report. Other teachers remarked that his failure to be sensible was holding him back. For the *Beyond the Grid* podcast Adrian was asked if he ever considered following his father into the veterinary practice.

'I loved going on farm visits with him. I'd sit on his knee when I was about six and do the steering wheel while he did the pedals. Then occasionally, when I was kind of a little bit older into my very early teens, if there was an operation at the weekend and the surgery nurses weren't around, then I would help him with the operation.

'I was handing my dad the utensils and trying not to faint. But the bit of my dad's make-up, or interest that did definitely rub off, was that he was a huge car enthusiast, so he had Mini Cooper S's and then Lotus Elans and so forth. He used to enjoy tinkering with them and modifying them.

'He had a small workshop in his garden, which had basic metalworking equipment and welding equipment. Using that workshop was probably quite key to me. When I was about eight to ten, I'd buy these 1:12 scale models. The first one was a 1967 [John] Surtees Honda, and then the second one was the Hill Lotus, the 49B. Those 1:12 scale models were great actually, because all the parts are labelled so you got the terminology. In assembling them, you started to understand how the chassis side of the car works. But by the time I was about 11, I started to become bored of building, effectively, other people's designs.

'So I started sketching my own designs and then used my dad's workshop to make the fold-up bits of aluminium and bits of fibreglass and so forth, to create these 1:12 scale models. The bits I couldn't make, like the tyres and the engine, I just cannibalised off the old models. Those long boring summer holidays, I would sketch away and then make it. Whilst of course I had absolutely no idea what I was doing, I think the practice of sketching and then turning that into a 3D object was great learning experience from a very young age.'

While at school, what he longed to do was get back home and into his father's workshop. Richard Newey bought the kit version of a Lotus Elan in 1968 and Adrian was on hand to watch and help him assemble it. A visit to the Racing Car Show at Olympia was followed in May 1972 by his first motorsport event, the Gold Cup at Oulton Park, a non-championship F1 race run from 1954, which dropped to F5000 and lower formulae as cars got quicker in the 1970s.

The impressionable 13-year-old saw a field made up of ten European Formula 5000 cars joined by eight Formula 1 cars on the grid. Denny Hulme won in a Yardley McLaren and lapped everyone except second-placed (and 1972 World Champion) Emerson Fittipaldi in a Lotus 72D. The highlight for Adrian was watching cars run through the compression dip from Lodge corner, through Deer Leap, and watch them spring up to take the start/finish straight.

Kart Tricks

Following in the footsteps of three generations of the Newey family, at 13 he was packed off to Repton School. Repton is a boarding school in Derbyshire, keen on its sports. Former Olympic champion Harold Abrahams, of *Chariots of Fire* fame, was an old boy, as were Roald Dahl and Christopher Isherwood. Jeremy Clarkson was two years below him. Unusually they didn't play rugby, which was the singular team sport in which he excelled at Emscote. 'I went to this very Dickensian public school which, I'll be honest, I absolutely hated every single day there.'

At Repton he retreated from the boredom of boarding

school by throwing himself into drawing and reading – the subject was always motor cars. He would read everything he could find, with an obligatory cover-to-cover read of *Autosport* every week. From making models he moved on to karts and during holidays visited the local Shenington kart track. But unlike so many karting dads, father Richard said if he wanted one of his own, he would have to work for it. 'He said, "Look, if you want to go karting, you're going to have to buy your own kart. I'll double your money." For every pound I earned, he would put a pound in. I started washing cars, doing the newspaper rounds, picking plums from the orchard and selling them outside the veterinary practice.'

BELOW LEFT: Like the author, Adrian's first live motorsport experience was the Gold Cup meeting at Oulton Park, featuring F1 and F5000 machinery.

BELOW: The Shenington Kart Racing Club track, near Banbury, is still going strong, next to the former RAF Edgehill.

His first machine was a wheezing 199cc Barlotti which proved to be disappointingly slow. Adrian managed to convince the teacher who ran the workshop at Repton that he should bring it to school so that he could work on it during evenings and weekends. Thus the boring hours were filled with a junior motorsport apprenticeship – rebuilding the engine, the gearbox, uprating the brakes. But after all that industry and hard work it was still at the back of the Shenington grid when he first took it to a race.

What he needed was a new chassis and a lighter, 210cc engine. The chassis building required welding skills and the very motivated schoolboy student booked himself a place on a ten-day British Oxygen Company course. 'It wasn't actually

the driving that really interested me. It was how to make the kart go faster. The welding course in North Birmingham was an hour's bus ride from Stratford where I grew up. I was about 15 when I did it so I got a bit of peer pressure from all the other guys on the course because I actually turned out to be reasonably good at welding and brazing, so I became the lecturer's pet, which I got a bit of flak for. It was actually a good lesson because it made me start to learn how to fit in. I developed my Brummie accent, which was quite easy.'

Armed with this new skill, he returned to Repton to build his new Mk2 kart complete with uprated engine, new chassis and an electronic ignition that he found details for in *Practical Electronics* magazine.

The kart's debut at Repton did not go well. The unsilenced two-stroke engine caused a mighty roar heard throughout the school grounds as Adrian drove it around paths near the chapel. When one of his friends was given a try he crashed it, badly bending the rear axle. The headmaster was not pleased. He banned the

LEFT: The Grade II-listed Pears School building at Repton, in Derbyshire, one of England's oldest public schools.

kart from any future appearances within the precincts of the school. It is ironic that while fellow Reptonian and global petrolhead Jeremy Clarkson was expelled from Repton for smoking and drinking, it was Newey, A, who was singled out for disruptive vehicle hooliganism.

And then there was the Greenslade concert.

The Repton fifth-formers sneaked bottles of booze into their summer term concert by Dave Greenslade's up-and-coming progressive rock band concealed in their flared trousers and got steadily drunk as the evening progressed. When the sound controller on the mixing desk nipped off in the middle of the set, an emboldened Adrian jumped up to the desk and pushed all the sliders to maximum, with ear-shattering consequences. Apart from the temporary assault on all the students' hearing (before the sound mixer got back to his desk), the noise cracked the ceramics holding the school's famous stained-glass windows. He was not going to be taking his A-levels there, unlike Clarkson who still managed to take and fail the majority of his. Despite a charm offensive from his mother, Adrian was expelled at 16.

Becoming a Brummie

His new place of education was the entirely free Warwickshire College of Further Education in Leamington Spa. While his classmates were riding 50cc Yamaha FS1E and Honda PC50 mopeds, Adrian was drawn to a bigger bike. After one term on the bus he managed to persuade his parents into buying him a Moto Morini 350 for the commute. Formula 1 may be full of teenage F2 and even F1 drivers today, but at school in the 1970s it was easy to gain hero status with a large motorbike, and at 17 years of age Adrian got one.

The teenage 'biker' joined a bike club, appropriately for his neck of the woods, called Shakespeare's Bikers, which met at the Cross Keys pub every week. All of a sudden he had an entrée into a new social life, his fellow bikers, and contact with girls. For a time his world became so bike-centric that he contemplated designing motorbikes as a career. A future visit to the Triumph factory would convince him that this was not the path; he found it utterly depressing with the workforce firmly stuck with 1950s' attitudes and work practices. When his beloved gran, Kath, died he used the money she had given him to upgrade from the Motor Morini to a superbike, the Ducati 900SS. His parents were furious at the choice, but at 18 he had become an instant motorcycle god. Ironically, it was a motorbike that would come in handy in securing his first Formula 1 job.

His career path towards F1 had long been settled, despite an artistic ability inherited from his mother, as he told Tom Clarkson (no relation to Jeremy). 'I was pretty good academically. The funny thing is that I was actually better at the arts than sciences, if anything. So the careers advisor at school said I should take art, which I was pretty good at. Recommendations were English and History, but I had no interest in doing Art, English and History. I was completely single-minded at that point of wanting to work in motor racing and design. I was very lucky, to be perfectly honest, because for most people it takes them a long time to find their vocation. But for whatever reason, I think with me it just clicked from that very young age.'

Along with karting there were further trips to watch F2 and F5000 races at Mallory Park. 'Actually seeing the cars, hearing them, smelling them, looking at them in great detail, and the paddock was completely open, so nobody minded this spotty little kid poking around. In fact, the opposite happened. A lot of them would actually explain what they were doing. That was without doubt key, combined with my attempts to go karting.'

In the meantime he had an OND (Ordinary National Diploma) to complete and pass. When he realised he would need a university degree to get a place in

BELOW: An example of a Lotus Elan sports car. Adrian's father owned three over the years – two of them bought in kit form. He gave one of them to Adrian as a wedding present.

BELOW RIGHT: An example of the Ducati 900SS that helped Adrian smooth his way into a job at Fittipaldi.

a Formula 1 team, his focus on academic work was sharpened considerably. From his thorough study of *Autosport* magazine he knew that both the Brabham and March teams used the Southampton University 25 per cent wind tunnel. That would give him the perfect opportunity to offer his services. The degree course he chose was aeronautics and not mechanical engineering. With faultless logic he reasoned that the study of aerodynamics and lightweight materials would be a lot more useful in an F1 team than a degree that propelled graduates towards Britain's struggling automotive industry.

University Challenge

Former sports car designer, Ian Reed, was instrumental in pointing Adrian in the right direction. It was he who had convinced his keen teenage correspondent that he needed a degree to be taken seriously by an F1 team. When Adrian's struggles with mathematics in his first year at Southampton left him on the verge of quitting his degree course, Ian Reed told him to grit his teeth and persist. Like so many university courses, the theory-laden first year was the least satisfying, particularly for a student who excelled on the practical side. If he had left without a degree, Reed told him, he would only ever be a draftsman. His mentor was now working at March Engineering as a chassis designer, so his opinion carried weight. Ironically Adrian would shadow Reed's career in also designing cars for the Indy series, though the student would become eminently more

successful than the master. He took extra lessons in maths and scraped through his first year at Southampton.

The second year involved far more hands-on application of theory and Adrian began to see light at the end of the wind tunnel. His third-year project, he felt certain, was going to be the thing that would get him noticed by F1 teams. He had been studying the aerodynamic effect of wings as part of the aeronautical degree. Wings give aeroplanes lift. When reversed they give F1 cars downforce. Wings had first appeared in the American sports car series of 1967, used by Jim Hall on his Chaparral. The 2C was the first Chaparral to use an in-car adjustable rear wing. Similar to the air-brake used in the Mercedes-Benz 300 SLR, it was designed to lie flat for low drag on the straights and could be tipped up for improved braking through corners.

F1 cars were quick to spot the speed advantage and by 1969 they had proliferated and grown to monstrous proportion, raised ugly and high on insubstantial struts that were prone to collapse. By the Monaco GP of 1969 they had been reined in and then banned, but their low-level use had become more sophisticated through the 1970s.

Then, in 1977, Formula 1's most innovative designer (for good and bad) Colin Chapman – the closest thing to a design hero that Adrian will admit to – introduced ground effect, where the curved underside of the car had the same aerodynamic effect as a wing. This was heightened by sealing the outer edges of the chassis with flexible skirts that helped glue cars to the road, providing there was an effective seal. Should that seal be broken in a bumpy, high-speed corner, then the sudden lack of downforce could result in a high-speed meeting with the barriers on the outside of the corner.

The Lotus 78 of 1977 introduced the concept and was perfected for 1978 with the Lotus 79, when Mario Andretti (who Adrian would go on to engineer in America) dominated the F1 championship to become the second American World Champion. It was a constant battle for the sport's governing body to reduce cornering speeds and it led to the raising of right heights to counteract ground effect, and ultimately its removal from F1 cars.

But whereas the pinnacle of motorsport had been quick to adopt ground effect, sports cars were less speedy on the uptake. Sensing an opportunity with the same thinking-out-of-the-box attitude that would make him a multiple championship winner, Adrian chose to make his final-year project at Southampton about the application of ground effect aerodynamics to sports cars.

BELOW: Jackie Stewart takes Copse corner in the 1973 British GP at Silverstone. Adrian was watching his first F1 grand prix from Woodcote.

He threw himself into it, making scale models to test in Southampton's wind tunnel, investing far more time than was merited for what would count towards 25 per cent of his degree. The final version of his design would have been an uncomfortable ride owing to the stiffness needed to employ ground effect, but it was a perfect demonstration of his practical and theoretical skills and showed he had a good insight into its application.

'It gave me something I could show to prospective employers and it contributed to my achieving a first-class honours degree,' he wrote in his autobiography, 'the very idea of which would have caused me to utter a four-letter expletive had it been suggested at Christmas of my first year.'

Now to find a job – which wasn't so easy. The idea of hanging out with the Brabham guys who were using the Southampton wind tunnel got him some friendly acquaintances, but no job offers. Closest to Colin Chapman in design-guru standing was Brabham's Gordon Murray, who had built an ingenious fan car in 1978. The Brabham BT46 complied with the sport's regulations because the fan was primarily there to cool the engine, but it also helped suck the car to the road. It romped to a first win in the Swedish GP of 1978 to the furore of the paddock. But like the double diffuser of 2009, it was legal. Brabham boss Bernie Ecclestone voluntarily withdrew this innovation to keep his fellow British teams onside in the bigger battle with the sport's governing body.

Adrian wrote to Gordon Murray with an extract from his sports car project, but the future designer of McLaren's F1 roadcar had no Brabham vacancies. Tyrrell offered him a place if he could find sponsorship – which he couldn't – and Lotus road cars in Norfolk seemed like his only option. Having helped build a Lotus

BELOW: Gordon Murray (left) with Brabham boss Bernie Ecclestone. Bernie would go on to sell his team in 1988.

RIGHT: Harvey Postlethwaite and Peter Warr standing over the Fittipaldi F8 of Emerson Fittipaldi at the 1980 British GP at Brands Hatch.

Elan, he was eminently employable but not enthused to go and work for a company responsible for the poor-quality Esprit and the ill-fated Delorean project. However it seemed like the only offer going. The alternative would have seen F1's greatest designer choose a completely different career path.

'I was actually on the verge of staying on to do a PhD on helicopter rotor blades,' he told journalist Adam Cooper, 'when Harvey Postlethwaite rang me up, a good two or three months after I'd written a letter to the Fittipaldi team.'

Harvey was the designer for the meteoric Hesketh racing team that catapulted James Hunt into the limelight and was a proven race-winning designer for the Wolf racing team. When Wolf sold the team to former World Champion Emerson Fittipaldi, Postlethwaite stayed on as designer. Harvey saw promise in the project notes that Adrian had sent him. Could he come for an interview...?

VALVOLINE
Bud
OF BEERS
3

Bud
KING OF BEERS
RED ROOF INNS
3
86
863
86
CHAMPION
USAC
Bud
KING OF BEERS
Bud
KING OF BEERS
GOODYEAR
Budweiser

2

MARCH TO AMERICA

PREVIOUS PAGE: The Indy 500-winning March 86C of Bobby Rahal.

LEFT: Keke Rosberg in the Fittipaldi F8C at the 1981 US Grand Prix West at Long Beach. Rosberg's best finish in 1981 for Fittipaldi was a ninth place in Brazil. The next year he was World Champion in a Williams.

Adrian turned up for his important Fittipaldi interview at the factory unit near Reading, not in a suit and tie, but in his biker leathers. Having followed F1 with an intense scrutiny through the early 1970s he was aware of Harvey Postlethwaite's race-winning Hesketh 308 and his even more successful Wolf WR1 which had taken Jody Scheckter to second place in the 1977 World Championship. Adrian had every reason to be nervous meeting a star of the F1 paddock. But the meeting got off to an unusual start.

'I remember turning up for the interview on a Ducati 900SS. Harvey had a Moto Guzzi Le Mans and the two bikes were great rivals at the time. Before we started on the interview he looked at the Ducati and asked if he could ride it. He went round the trading estate on it and I think we spent the first hour chatting about bikes rather than cars. It was a good start.' And a good finish. 'He offered me a job the next day.'

Newey soon got involved on the new Fittipaldi F8, introduced at mid-season. 'I was joining the aerodynamics team as Junior Aerodynamicist. What I didn't realise was that I was going to be the whole aerodynamics team. The F8 was quite a good car, but there was little money for development.'

For 1981 the FIA had moved the skirt regulations for ground effect – they now had to be 6cm off the ground – and so the 1981 cars were mostly the 1980 models with less effective rubber skirts.

The Junior Aerodynamicist's idea was to raise the underwing of the 1982 car, which was being developed in 1981, so that the leakage of airflow under the skirts was minimised. Together with a Fittipaldi fabricator, Adrian would bundle a load of models plus ad hoc bits into a Vauxhall Chevette van and head off to the Imperial College wind tunnel in Kensington to test out his theories. He was on the brink of manufacturing the attendant suspension system to accommodate his new designs when the budget was withdrawn.

With sponsors pulling out, work on the 1982 car came to a halt; the team would have to use the 1981 model. In 1981 the drivers were Brazilian Chico Serra and the man destined to become the 1982 World Champion, Keke Rosberg. For 1982 it would only be Serra driving the Fittipaldi.

Key staff began to leave: Harvey went off to work for Ferrari, Peter Warr headed to Lotus and Peter Macintosh to March. His colleagues clearly had a good idea of Newey's potential. He had an offer from Warr to move to the Lotus F1 team, and one from Macintosh to join March, who were then building GT and customer IndyCars for the American market, as well as Formula 2 machinery.

ABOVE: Harvey Postlethwaite – seen here talking to James Hunt at Watkins Glen in 1975 – made his reputation at Hesketh and subsequently at Walter Wolf Racing.

ABOVE RIGHT: Emerson Fittipaldi with his drivers, Chico Serra and Keke Rosberg, before the San Marino Grand Prix in 1981.

March Engineering

Adrian took the less glamorous route, feeling that he would get greater experience at a production race car builder like March – another shrewd move. March Engineering had been founded in 1969 by Max Mosley, Alan Rees, Graham Coaker and Robin Herd. MARCH was an acronym of their initials. They each had a specific area of expertise: lawyer Mosley looked after the commercial side, Rees managed the racing team, Coaker oversaw production at the factory in Bicester, Oxfordshire, and Herd was the designer.

Most would have jumped at the chance to progress in grand prix racing, especially under the wing of Colin Chapman at Lotus, but Adrian preferred the traditional 'jack of all trades' apprenticeship that the likes of designers Patrick Head and John Barnard also experienced at March's great rivals, Lola.

To start off with, Macintosh offered Adrian the chance to work on the March Formula 2 team in a race-engineering role and through the week as a draughtsman in the March office. Race-engineering was a discipline he

understood but had never practised, rarely attending Fittipaldi tests.

Peter Warr had similarly recognised his great potential and offered him a job as an aerodynamicist at Lotus – it was the chance to rub shoulders with Colin Chapman (before his untimely heart attack in 1982). Given this was the team that had capitalised on ground effect, it had been a tempting offer.

Newey's pragmatic choice would help define his future career and give him the unique grounding he has used to create championship-winning cars. He has often pointed out that today's designers have a far more specialised job spec. In Formula 1 there are three departments. There is the aerodynamics department, there is the design office and there is race-engineering and, 'nobody crosses from one department to the other'.

His baptism of fire came in March 1982, the start of the Formula 2 season at Silverstone. The March team was running three cars – Corrado Fabi (brother of Teo), ex-motorbike World Champion Johnny Cecotto, and Adrian was engineering Christian Danner. It was a wet race, but Danner took the lead, set fastest lap and was heading for victory until ... his car ran out of fuel. Back in the garage he unleashed a full-blown Germanic tirade against his incompetent

ABOVE: The inelegant shovel front of 'HMS Budweiser' otherwise known as the March 817.

ABOVE RIGHT: The March GTP car, the 83G. In the hands of Al Holbert it won the 1983 IMSA Camel GT Championship. It also won the 1984 Daytona 24-Hour race with its new owners, the South African-based 'Kreepy Krauly' team.

rookie race engineer and fired him on the spot. It was only later that the team discovered there had been a fuel leak prompting the retirement.

The ever-helpful Cecotto suggested that he swap race engineers with Danner and so for the next round at Hockenheim, Adrian engineered the Venezuelan – to a fourth place, as it happened. At the third round of the season, Thruxton, Cecotto won. His faith in Newey was reinforced later in the year at Pau, the Monaco-like street track in the south of France. Walking the track, the rookie engineer came to the conclusion that the bumpy circuit would need soft springs to absorb the undulations and keep the tyre contact patch on the road surface. In one of the earliest manifestations of Adrian's ultra-competitive nature, he concealed his set-up changes from the rest of the team and hid the remaining soft springs in the transporter so Fabi and Danner were stuck with the stiffer factory settings. Cecotto won and would go on to finish second to Fabi in the championship in a season when March won eight of the 13 races.

Back in the design department Adrian was put to work on March's 1983 Can-Am sports car, the March 817, marrying an F1 chassis to big, slab-like bodywork designed by Max Sardou. The unloved machine was known jauntily as 'HMS Budweiser' in tribute to the highly visible sponsor on the highly visible bodywork. Newey had little faith in the design but was too new to the team to make his opinion count.

Not content to be so easily bypassed, he formulated plans for another Sardou design, the March-Chevrolet 82G sports car that had competed and failed to finish at Le Mans. The March factory entry had lasted ten hours, 78 laps, while the Truesports customer car of Bobby Rahal and Jim Trueman disappeared after seven hours, completing just 28 laps.

This time Adrian decided to go straight to the boss of March, Robin Herd. Herd himself was a brilliant engineer and designer having worked on the Concorde supersonic jet project and designed race-winning McLarens, including the McLaren M7 for Denny Hulme. Herd listened to the planned changes and took on board Newey's knowledge of sports car design from his university project ... and gave him the go-ahead. Though the caveats were that he could have no wind tunnel time and no design support – Adrian would have to do everything by eye and use his limited experience.

His competitive side immediately rose to the surface. Newey managed to shed a substantial 40kg of weight from the car and, by redesigning the Sardou aerodynamics and producing a new underwing, gave the sports car more downforce and better balance. The car was re-christened the 83G and packed off to compete at the 1983 Daytona 24-hour race. Adrian was packed off to engineer it.

85
MOBILE BAY REFINING
FARM STORES
Spirit of Miami
BOSCH
Hoosier

16
Bud
CIBIE

LEFT: A March 84G that was once driven by Adrian's former boss Emerson Fittipaldi at the 1985 Miami Grand Prix GTP race along with local sports car hero Tony Garcia.

BELOW LEFT: The March 84G was conventionally powered by a Chevrolet V8 but it also ran with a Buick V6, a Porsche flat-six, and was once fitted with a Mazda rotary engine.

Daytona 24 Hours

And so in late January 1983, the now-bearded 24-year-old suddenly found himself running an IMSA GTP car in a 24-hour race. He had grown the beard simply to look more experienced.

'The car was finished about a week before the race, and I went with it, along with two or three mechanics from March,' he told journalist Adam Cooper. 'We arrived to find that the guy Robin had sold the car to was a wealthy American who reckoned he was pretty good in his Ferrari road car, and fancied a go at Daytona. We managed to persuade him that this wasn't a good idea. He had a couple of reasonable drivers, Marty Hinze and Randy Lanier, and a third driver, Terry Wolters, turned up who was completely myopic, with spectacles like milk bottles.

'We started the race, and I sort of assumed the role of team manager because there wasn't anybody else. We had no timing system so we didn't know where we were in the order. We'd been working through the night before the race so were dog-tired, and the feeling was that it didn't really matter; we reckoned it would break down two hours into the race and then we could all go home.'

Things didn't go to plan and the car continued pounding round.

'We got to about 1am and the thing was still going when I went off for a break. Like at Indianapolis, Daytona has this tower with all these numbers on it, and 88 was at the top. I thought, "That looks familiar". I dashed back to the pits and, sure enough, we were 88. We actually led until it rained and we got water in the distributor cap at about 8am, but we eventually finished second.'

After the race, the happy but exhausted March mechanics bundled into a Chevrolet hire car and headed back to the hotel. Everyone fell asleep, including the driver, who rolled forward at a stop light and was T-boned by another car. All survived, but it was a rare example of a motorsport team wrecking a hire car completely by accident. Back in Bicester, an impressed Robin Herd allocated some budget so that Adrian could test his modifications in a wind tunnel.

Scheduled in late January/early February, the Daytona race gave potential buyers time to assess the merits of the Lola and March sports cars for the year ahead. When Porsche were unable to make their 956 eligible for the IMSA GTP sports car series in 1983, Al Holbert ordered a March 83G chassis. Holbert owned a Porsche dealership and wanted the March engineers to adapt the car to fit a Porsche engine. Clearly upset by the turn of events, Porsche refused to supply any engine or gearbox drawings to the March team and so Holbert had

ABOVE AND LEFT: Al Unser's championship-winning 1985 Penske Racing March 85C. This particular car was sold in 2024 by Sotheby's in Hershey, Pennsylvania, along with its Cosworth V8, for $71,500.

to buy the engine units and ship them to England where they could be measured and drawn. Newey stepped up to the challenge of redesigning the back of the chassis and the rear suspension to fit and by May it was ready to run in Charlotte, North Carolina. In practice the turbo was running too hot and with no time for a proven fix, Holbert turned up the boost for one hot lap to snatch P1 in qualifying, and during the race ran it as low as possible. It was a flag-to-flag victory, Adrian's first in North America. Holbert dominated the second half of the 1983 GTP championship with the season culminating in victory at the final race, the shorter 3 Hours of Daytona.

In the summer of 1983 Adrian also found time to marry his girlfriend Amanda, a nurse who had been working in Bath. Their time together would have implications for any move to Ferrari in the future.

IndyCar

The following year, 1984, would be another steep learning curve – both professionally and emotionally. He had now race-engineered in Formula 2 and GTP. Even though Daytona was an oval speedway, the 24-hour race runs through the infield very much like Formula 1 when it ran at Indianapolis. For 1984 he would be tackling a wide variety of ovals with an IndyCar, an entirely new discipline.

Robin Herd had touted Newey to the Truesports team as a 'promising young engineer'. The team would have been well aware that he had been able to transform the woeful 82G they had tanked with at Le Mans from an ugly duckling into a race-winning machine.

Adrian would develop the Ralph Bellamy-designed March 84C IndyCar through the summer of 1984 in close cooperation with driver Bobby Rahal. It was the detailed feedback that Rahal was able to give Adrian which allowed engineer and driver to improve the performance of a 'clumsy' chassis, lagging behind its rival Lola. By the end of the season the March was able to challenge the Lola – in the hands of Mario Andretti – for wins. Rahal won two of the last three races, but more importantly the season had helped build a strong bond between Rahal and Newey.

Things were not so good for Amanda who had moved to the States with Adrian, but failed to find a substitute for the nursing career she had left behind. It didn't help that they were living in a 'soulless' condo near the Truesports facility in quiet Columbus, Ohio. She arrived in the spring but by July had returned home to their cottage near Chippenham in Wiltshire.

LEFT: Because of his relative inexperience as a race engineer, when Adrian got to the United States he grew a beard. Here he checks the suspension of Bobby Rahal's 84C.

BELOW: This March 86C chassis won the 1986 Indy 500 for Bobby Rahal, though Newey was no longer engineering the car.

Adrian's previous work was still achieving results. Having transformed the March 83G sports car into a championship-winning machine it was renamed the 84G and won the 1984 IMSA GTP championship, this time in the hands of Randy Lanier. That particular car would have a notorious ending. Lanier's March was subsequently impounded by the US authorities after his conviction for drug trafficking and eventually sold by the US government four years later.

In England, the designers at March were being shuffled around. After Formula 2 was jettisoned for the new Formula 3000, Ralph Bellamy was moved on to create the new F3000 car for 1985. This left the way clear for Adrian to design his first car from scratch, the March IndyCar for 1985, the 85C. Having served time as an aerodynamicist and as an engineer he was in the perfect position to marry both disciplines. It is one of the fundamental reasons he has been so successful in his career as he acknowledged in his autobiography.

'What it gives me is the insight to approach a design from a holistic point of view, avoiding the situation where you see a car

where clearly the aerodynamicist and the chief designer were having a row, since you've either got nasty mechanical bits sticking out of what was otherwise a clean aerodynamic surface or an elegantly-looking car that performs poorly, because it has the stiffness of a rubber band.'

Though it was the perfect opportunity for Newey to show off his skillset, the design process was not ideal. While he was engineering Rahal to third place in the 1984 CART IndyCar series, he was flying backwards and forwards across the Atlantic designing the March 85C.

'It won't go down as one of the cars I'm particularly proud of, but it was my first clean-sheet-of-paper car. Unfortunately, the 85C was done while commuting, so I didn't have time to do it properly.'

First Designs: The March 85C and 86C

Indeed, it was an inauspicious start. Mirroring 1984, Rahal's early results were woeful, the Ohioan finishing 27th, 27th, 9th, 20th, 25th and 28th in his first six outings. The omens didn't look good. But Truesports weren't the only team running the March 85C. Danny Sullivan, driving for Team Penske, pulled off one of the most remarkable victories in the second race of the season, which just happened

to be the Indianapolis 500. It was the 69th running of the great race and became one of the most famous, featuring Sullivan's 'Spin to Win' where he passed and spun in front of leader Mario Andretti's Lola, but failed to hit anything concrete.

Despite the tyre wear, Sullivan went on to win his only Indy 500 and further embellish Newey's North American motorsport CV. Sadly for the Rahal/Newey partnership, Bobby's wins didn't come until the latter half of the season, the Truesports car eventually finishing third in the championship.

Piling on the glory, Al Unser in the Penske March 85C managed to win the CART championship by a single point from his son Al Unser Jr in the Lola 900. March also won the CART Constructors' Cup. A car Adrian was 'not particularly proud of' had managed to win the Indy 500, claim first and third in the drivers' championship and win the Constructors' Cup. For the modest 'Brummie' with an indecipherable accent to Americans, 1985 was a good year for another reason. He had been able to start on the following season's car, the 86C, early giving him precious time in the wind tunnel.

The following season would be different. Adrian would now be attached to the Kraco team as race engineer for Michael Andretti, who would be driving his March 86C. Son of Mario, Michael Andretti was a promising driver who would later make a move to join Formula 1, partnering Ayrton Senna at McLaren. The up-and-coming designer from the Midlands was thrilled to be joining a team based in Los Angeles, with a condo on glamorous Hermosa Beach. No matter that the team was based in the scary district of Compton nearby, this was West Coast. Adrian never failed to reflect that had things gone a different way in his career he could have been stress-testing door hinges on a Morris Marina at British Leyland in Birmingham.

For a committed workaholic, the 1986 season would be one that tested Newey's capacity to the limit. He started off engineering the Kraco March 86C and began to have tentative plans for what would be the 87C. In the 'Month of May' he was pleased to see his friend Bobby Rahal take Indy 500 victory in another March 86C – making it two successive wins. Ironically the Truesports team with Rahal driving would provide Michael Andretti's biggest competition that year.

RIGHT: Two views of Bobby Rahal's 1986 Indianapolis 500-winning March 86C. He also claimed the 1986 CART IndyCar series in an 86C.This car, auctioned by Sotheby's, is still equipped with its original Indy-winning Cosworth DFX V-8.

Team Haas

Then, in July, former McLaren team boss Teddy Mayer came calling. Mayer had been the boss of the successful McLaren team of the 1970s which had propelled James Hunt to the 1976 drivers' title. He had been hired by Carl Haas (no relation

VALVOLINE
Bud
Bud
Bud
3

momo
march

to Gene Haas of the current grid) to manage a team backed by Ford and US food company Beatrice, a long-established IndyCar sponsor. Newey was anxious to get back to Formula 1 after his brief foray with Fittipaldi and accepted a role as technical director. Beatrice were sponsoring a Team Haas Lola chassis, the THL2, with drivers Patrick Tambay and Alan Jones, but it would be Newey who would be designing their 1987 car. Or would he...?

Robin Herd agreed to release Adrian early, mindful of his desire to get back to F1, but insisted that he finish the season race-engineering Michael Andretti. At the same time Teddy Mayer thought it would be good to have Adrian embed himself in the Beatrice-sponsored team by race-engineering Patrick Tambay. In addition he had to design the 1987 F1 car. Thus Adrian spent his time on a plane to US CART races, to F1 races, and in between heading for the Beatrice Haas design office at Colnbrook, handily near Heathrow. His first daughter,

Charlotte, was born on 28 August 1986 – three days before the Mid-Ohio IndyCar race, eleven days after the Austrian Grand Prix and ten days before the Italian Grand Prix. He was aware he was spinning too many plates.

The joy of fatherhood was tempered by an unmanageable workload. Working at Team Haas Lola (THL) at the time was ex-Williams designer Neil Oatley (who would go on to work alongside John Barnard at McLaren), and aerodynamicist Ross Brawn.

'It was certainly a very talented drawing office,' he told Adam Cooper. 'Unfortunately the management style of Teddy Mayer seemed to be to tell Ross Brawn, Neil Oatley and myself that we were the boss, and then let us fight it out. The atmosphere wasn't as congenial as it might have been, and it isn't a period I look back on with any fondness.'

With ill-defined roles Adrian came up against his first creative block for the 1987 THL3 (the team was also known as FORCE, Formula One Race Car Engineering), something that was a huge concern to such an innovative mind. He had imagined he might be joining the collaborative esprit de corps of the old March team, but found himself mired in office politics. So it was a temporary relief when he learned that the team was being wound up in November. He had come in at the tail end of what had been an expensive venture and yet another salutary lesson, that throwing money at an F1 team is never guaranteed to bring results.

ABOVE: The Beatrice-backed Haas-Lola team had some talented design personnel and top drivers (Patrick Tambay and Alan Jones) but folded before realising any of its potential.

LEFT: Having designed Daytona- and Indy 500-winning race cars by 1986, Adrian decided to ditch the beard.

However, the movers and shakers of F1 were aware that a designer of Newey's quality would soon be available. He got a call out of the blue from Bernie Ecclestone, who apart from organising the FOCA (Formula One Constructors Association) teams was also the owner of the Brabham team. His star designer, Gordon Murray (the man who had designed World Championship-winning Brabhams for Nelson Piquet), was leaving to join McLaren. How would Adrian feel about moving to Chessington in Surrey and replacing him?

The Brabham move never came to be. Before Adrian could take up the offer he got a call from Bernie letting him know that he would be selling the team, as his new focus would be the commercial exploitation of F1. He could opt out. Having seen what happened with the unstable finances of Fittipaldi and then FORCE/Beatrice/Team Haas Lola, Adrian chose to suspend his F1 ambitions and take up a role back in the States.

Carl Haas was the North American importer for Lola cars. Though Roger Penske also built chassis for the series, Lola was the March team's main opposition. Apart from dabbling in F1, Carl also ran his own IndyCar team alongside movie-star petrolhead Paul Newman. The Newman-Haas operation was a leading team in the CART championship with star driver Mario Andretti.

The offer that the cigar-chomping Haas tabled for Adrian's services was eye-watering. Newey had earned $60,000 looking after Michael Andretti at Kraco – for 1987 he would earn $400,000 as race engineer for Mario making him possibly the world's highest-paid race engineer. There was a logic to the financial lure – the Newey-configured March cars had won both the CART championship and the Indy 500 in 1985 and 1986. With Adrian's talent for race optimisation applied to the Lola in 1987, not only would the Newman/Haas team be gaining from his expertise, they would be denying March the re-employment of their talismanic figure (that is, if you could be a talisman aged 28).

Apart from race-engineering an icon of American motorsport, Newey had to design a new front end to the gearbox so that the Lola T87 could accommodate a new Chevrolet engine. The engine was put together by Mario Illien and Paul Morgan, the 'Il' and 'Mor' of Ilmor, in Brixworth, Northamptonshire. Ilmor would go on to build successful engines for McLaren and Mercedes, and would be an organisation that Adrian would work closely with in the future.

Despite developing a strong relationship with Mario Andretti through the course of the season, 1987 did not bring success for Newman/Haas. Andretti is both a brave and resilient driver, but plagued with ill-luck, very much in the way that Rubens Barrichello took all the Ferrari bad luck in his years alongside Michael Schumacher. Mario was one lap ahead of the field in the Indy 500 with 50 miles to go, cruising to easy victory when a resonance in the engine made it drop a

BELOW LEFT: Bobby Rahal winning at Indianapolis in 1986. The March 86C also won the 1987 Indianapolis 500 in the hands of Al Unser making it three Indy wins in a row.

BELOW: Mario Andretti in the Newman/Haas Lola leads son Michael Andretti in the Kraco Racing, March 86C on the streets of Long Beach in 1986.

cylinder and his race was over. He won twice in 1987, but would only finish sixth in the standings. Nevertheless, Carl Haas's enthusiasm for having Adrian in the race team was undimmed and he held onto the hope that Newey would get involved in designing the 1988 Lola.

While he had been involved in his American adventures, the large Japanese department store Leyton House, owned by Akira Akagi, had taken the first steps into Formula 1 with a March-built car. In reality the 1987 car was an F3000 chassis with an F1 engine bolted on, but its debut had given Korean national Akagi the first taste of the Formula 1 circus and he wanted a proper car for 1988. And so in the summer of 1987 Adrian was approached by Robin Herd of March with the offer of a job, to create the 1988 Leyton House March. Would he be interested? Step forward Warwickshire College of Further Education's greatest engineering alumnus.

3

BP
LEYTON HOUSE
BP
Marlboro
LEYTON HOUSE
CARGLASS
ANIBEL
ANIBEL
LEYTON HOUSE
BP
16

LEYTON HOUSE MARCH

PREVIOUS PAGE: Ivan Capelli drives the Leyton House March CG891 during the French Grand Prix at the Circuit Paul Ricard in 1989.

LEFT: The Leyton House factory unit in Bicester pictured in 1989. The contrast between this and the 2025 Aston Martin Campus at Silverstone could not be more extreme.

Very few F1 teams are named after areas of London's East End – Leyton House was reportedly named after Leyton in east London because its Korean owner spent time there. Although a competing theory is that it was named after the London art museum Leighton House. His successful Japanese company started life investing in property, subsequently moving into the department store business. The glamorous world of Formula 1 was the perfect promotional vehicle with a Japanese public fully engaged with the sporting success of Honda F1 engines in the 1980s.

Adrian moved from being one of the world's highest-paid racing engineers to one of the least-remunerated technical directors with a salary of £140,000. When he arrived at Bicester, he found the March F1 team removed from the F3000 and IndyCar factory with its own industrial unit.

Formula 1 technical regulations were about to change, always the best time for an innovative or radical approach. The massive power of the 1.5-litre, V6 turbo era was going to be replaced by cheaper, normally aspirated engines with 3.5 litres – though 1988 would be a transition year with both engines on the grid. In 1989 the turbos would be banned, leaving just normally aspirated V8s.

Robin Herd set Newey's target for 1988 to be the best of the 3.5-litre cars. Ever the competitor, Adrian set his goal as mixing it with the turbos. He had good reason to be optimistic – whereas the turbo cars had been able to produce 1,300 bhp in 1987, they would be restricted to 900 bhp in 1988.

He also reasoned that the turbo teams had become lazy in their approach, simply bolting on bigger front and rear wings and letting the engine power mask the attendant

drag. 'In the turbo era the main way to make your car go quick was give it more boost and put bigger and bigger rear wings on,' he told *Motor Sport*'s Marcus Simmons. 'They'd pretty much ignored aero efficiency.'

His mission in designing the Leyton House March 881 was to create a light, aerodynamically efficient car that made the most of their Judd engine's 580 bhp. He wrote in his autobiography: 'In terms of providing a template for future designs, it was probably the most important of my career.'

ABOVE: Ivan Capelli at La Source hairpin in his March-Judd 881 during the 1988 Belgian Grand Prix. Capelli finished in fifth place but was later given third after third and fourth were disqualified.

It was his first 'clean sheet of paper' Formula 1 car, based around their single driver from 1987, Ivan Capelli. Capelli, who would go on to race for Ferrari in 1992, was a smallish guy and Adrian planned to use this to his advantage, designing as tight a chassis around the cockpit tub as was possible. This V-shape gave a minimal cross-section. He also curved the front-wing endplates around the front tyres – until that time, the norm had been to end the front wing in front of the tyre, so it didn't interfere with steering lock. The driver's pedals were raised off the floor, so the nose of the car could be sculpted underneath. These were just some of the elements he brought to bear in his first F1 design, and their effectiveness can be judged by their widespread adoption across the grid.

'In many ways it's one of the cars I'm still proudest of, because it completely changed the design direction of F1. Although the Tyrrell of a few years later (1990) was credited with being the first raised-nose car it was actually the March — we raised the nose underneath and tried to make it an extension of the front wing.

'We sat Ivan in the mock-up and kept moving the pedals towards him and said, "How far can we go for you still to be comfortable and drive the car?" He came up with a number and we built it to that number, but when he came to drive it he was a bit squashed. It was due to our inexperience and his that it was too small.'

The improvement in downforce for the car was a quantum leap from that of its F1 predecessor, the March 871. The model was duly tested back at the Southampton University wind tunnel and the results were promising. It needed to be ready for testing in February 1988, but the design process from July 1987 onwards was regularly interrupted by obligatory trips back to the US for Adrian to complete his season with Newman/Haas. The continued engineering of Mario Andretti had been a condition of his release from Carl Haas, along with not working on any March IndyCars.

Testing at Imola began with the grandee teams, Ferrari, McLaren, Williams et al, keen to see if this remarkable new car could actually go fast. Harvey Postlethwaite even crawled underneath a half-closed March garage door to get a better look. It might have gone fast if Ivan Capelli were able to change gear. One of the recurring criticisms of Newey's cars, particularly by engineers, is that he packages things too tightly which leads to overheating. In this instance, the driver-hugging cockpit was so constrained that Capelli couldn't move his hand to change gear.

To fix the problem March cut a hole in the side of the cockpit and widened it until it was big enough for Ivan to operate the gear lever. The technical director then turned fabricator, making a mould of the blister and then creating a new carbon-fibre version overnight which he attached to the car and painted in Leyton House team colours. It was an epic 'save' from an epic oversight.

However, the four-day test was beset with gearbox problems that limited extensive running. Even so, the team had already proven that they were the fastest of the 3.5-litre cars.

The early-season results were not as successful as the tests had promised. It looked like they had flattered to deceive. Gearbox issues were the principal mechanical issue behind the DNFs. When that was fixed courtesy of a tip-off from a Williams engineer who recommended they try a David Brown Engineering gearbox, the potential of the car could finally be unleashed ... But even at tracks such as Monaco, where power is less important than handling, Leyton House failed to achieve a balanced set-up. The car was suffering from low-speed, mid-corner understeer.

ABOVE: Ivan Capelli (left) and Brazilian Mauricio Gugelmin photographed before the start of testing at Estoril in 1989.

ABOVE RIGHT: Mauricio Gugelmin at a rain-soaked Hungaroring in 1988.

RIGHT: The gear lever 'blister' on the bodywork is prominent on this CG891 of 1989.

LEYTON
march
LEYTON HOUSE
15
PERDIGAO

BP
AUTOGLASS
LEYTON HOUSE

Results continually failed to arrive, the drivers (Capelli had been teamed up with the slightly more bulky Mauricio Gugelmin) were regularly complaining of understeer. The gloom was only lifted by their first points-paying position of the season in June's Canadian GP, a fifth place for Capelli. In the 1980s, with points being restricted to the top six, that was a significant two points and fulfilled Newey's ambition of being the first of the normally aspirated cars.

Nevertheless he was unhappy that the March wasn't regularly beating the likes of AGS, Minardi, Tyrrell, Dallara and Williams, the latter of which had the same Judd V8 as the March 881. They all struggled to beat the Benetton, which had exclusive use of the Cosworth DFR engine – the rest of the grid could only buy the Cosworth DFZ.

After the French Grand Prix Leyton House started to build momentum. At the old Hockenheim, a long power blast through the trees, Capelli qualified seventh, ahead of the turbo-powered Lotus-Honda of Satoru Nakajima (albeit four seconds behind Senna on pole for McLaren) and finished the race in fifth place. The following race Ivan qualified on the second row of the grid, heady stuff. Newey had introduced a longer nose and a new front wing, and although Capelli retired with engine problems, Gugelmin took another fifth place.

The highlight of the season came at the 1988 Portuguese Grand Prix in Estoril when Ivan Capelli took third place on the grid, only beaten by the two McLaren MP4/4 cars that would sweep 15 of 16 victories in that all-conquering year. It was no fluke, Mauricio Gugelmin took fifth as well. In the race it got even better; Prost led the race, but Capelli was able to harry the McLaren of Ayrton Senna until finally he got past the great Brazilian as well as bringing home the first Leyton House podium.

It was a grand prix weekend in which Alain Prost had been astonished by the downforce levels generated by the March 881 in practice. 'I do remember Ivan coming round with Prost trawling along behind him in third gear and then accelerating again,' Adrian recalled. 'I thought, "What on earth is he doing?" It turns out that the entry speed Ivan carried into that long,180-degree final corner, Prost was convinced he was going to crash and he didn't want to get tangled up in the accident, so he backed right off.'

On to the penultimate grand prix in Japan, a wet race at Suzuka in which Senna had stalled to the back of the grid and came storming through. As he was recovering through the field Ivan Capelli was threatening to overtake the leading McLaren of Alain Prost, who was hampered by a malfunctioning gearbox. On Lap 16 Capelli seized his chance to pass Prost when the Frenchman missed a gear exiting the chicane. The Leyton House March took the lead, the first time a non-turbo car had led a grand prix since 1983! Capelli's time in front only lasted the length of the straight, as the extra power of the Honda turbo engine allowed Prost to surge past going into the first turn. Capelli made further attempts to overtake Prost before retiring three laps later with what was described at the time as 'electrical failure'. A year later and Ivan finally admitted that he might have knocked the ignition switch off by mistake when trying to adjust the rear anti-roll bar lever.

LEFT: With the 1989 car – the CG891 – only being introduced at the Monaco Grand Prix, the team decked out the 881, complete with the new livery, for the first two races of the year in Brazil and Imola. Gugelmin drove the 881 to third place at his home race in Brazil.

It had been a year that had matched the Newey expectations – they had beaten the other normally aspirated cars, the only exception being the Benetton-

Cosworth DFR. This special-build engine was superficially a DFV-design, but almost the only feature carried over from previous Cosworth models was the basic 90-degree V8 engine architecture. The March 881 had also mixed it with the turbo cars and finished just a single point behind Lotus-Honda and Arrows-Megatron. If only Ivan hadn't switched the ignition off they might have finished fourth in the constructors' championship.

RIGHT: Mauricio Gugelmin describes the handling of his CG891 to team-mate Capelli at Monaco in 1989, while Adrian ponders.

BELOW: Ivan Capelli sweeps round the Old Station/Loews Hotel/Fairmont Hairpin at Monaco in 1990.

1989 Setbacks

The following year brought a series of challenges. Although Adrian became a father for the second time in February 1989, another daughter, Hannah, it was a rare happy moment. There were irreparable fracture lines in his marriage.

The Leyton House March 891 was late through a series of problems – cracks in the gearbox casing, a regularly seizing fuel pump due to flexing bodywork. It was so unreliable that the previous year's car was used for the first two races, at

Brazil and Imola, and the 1989 car only made its debut at Monaco.

It was badged as the CG891 in tribute to Cesare Gariboldi, the Italian manager of Ivan Capelli who enjoyed an almost father-and-son-like relationship with his driver, as well as mentoring other F1 drivers such as Teo and Corrado Fabi and Bruno Giacomelli. When Gariboldi was killed in a road crash in January 1989, 'the spark went out of Ivan for a time,' recalled March team boss Ian Phillips. 'Cesare was a great person to have around and he was the key to Ivan. He could translate what he wanted to the engineers.'

Inevitably there was increased competition from the midfield F1 teams who had copied features from the March 881: the V-shaped monocoque and, most conspicuous of all, the raised nose. Added to that, Newey bemoaned a new Judd engine that was underpowered, up against newer offerings from Honda and Renault who had built V10 engines for 1989, plus Ford had released the Cosworth DFR to all its customers.

Ivan Capelli managed to claim a second row of the grid spot for the fourth race of the season, the Mexican Grand Prix, but he went to the grid leaking brake fluid and retired on Lap 1. That would be one of 14 retirements in a disastrous 16-race season in which his best result was an 11th place. Mauricio Gugelmin managed to score a podium in the first race, but that was with the March 881; after that the highest he finished was P7.

Marriage aside, what was most troubling to Newey in 1989 was that he couldn't get to the bottom of the handling and aerodynamic issues of the car. The inconsistencies carried through to the 1990 car, the CG901. And the team was still going backwards. At Mexico in June, both cars failed to qualify.

At this point the Leyton House team were using two wind tunnels – one recently established by Robin Herd, Comtec in Brackley, at 40 per cent, and the smaller, familiar wind tunnel in Southampton at 25 per cent. Adrian's lightbulb moment came when he noticed that the wind tunnels were giving very different results.

'Amazingly we hadn't realised that beneath the rolling road [at Southampton] the aluminium plates had a wooden centre core that had started distorting with heat. So it was getting more and more bowed. We finally realised it in the spring of 1990, put it right and redeveloped the aerodynamics.'

Two weeks after they had failed to qualify for Mexico, Ivan Capelli was leading the French Grand Prix at Paul Ricard, with Mauricio Gugelmin behind. Gugelmin retired with engine problems, but Capelli fought a heroic rearguard action to fend off Prost's Ferrari until three laps before the end. Yet again, so close to a victory.

However, neither Adrian Newey nor team boss Ian Phillips were in the South of France to witness at first hand the spectacular effectiveness of the new diffuser that had solved so many of the car's issues.

At the Brazilian Grand Prix in March, team boss Ian Phillips had been taken ill with meningitis and was confined to a darkened home for his recovery. With Phillips absent Akagi – who had bought the F1 team off Robin Herd – promoted an accountant to run Leyton House.

BELOW: Ivan Capelli on the streets of Phoenix for the 1989 United States Grand Prix.

BELOW RIGHT: Mauricio Gugelmin demonstrates the robustness of the March chassis in spectacular fashion at the 1989 French GP at Paul Ricard.

'Akagi was starting to struggle financially,' Newey told Marcus Simmons. 'He borrowed heavily against the banks but had to be seen to be still in Formula 1, because if he pulled out, the banks would have wondered why. He was playing a poker game on the minimum cost possible, so he was reducing the budget constantly and brought in an accountant (Simon Keeble). When Ian had meningitis Keeble suddenly assumed power and that really was the beginning of the end — having an accountant running an F1 team was a disaster. He and I fell out in a big way.'

There were many shouting matches – and so Newey started to consider the approaches made from rival teams. No doubt alerted by the F1 rumour mill, former-driver-now-boss of Arrows, Jackie Oliver, offered him the role of technical

director. At the same time, co-owner of Williams, Patrick Head, asked him if he fancied a job as Head of Research and Development. Williams were proven World Champions, Arrows had yet to win a race. Tired of sticking his head above the parapet, Adrian chose to go to Williams.

He had yet to inform the boss when he walked into the office the Monday before the French GP. 'I was asked into Simon Keeble's office,' he related in his autobiography. 'He informed me that he had hired Chris Murphy, a designer from Lola as technical director, with Akagi's blessing (so it was claimed). I was therefore free either to accept a lesser role with the team and "carry on fiddling in the wind tunnel" or to leave. Effectively I was sacked.'

As sporting hiring and firing goes it was a decision right up there with the Portland Trail Blazers passing up the opportunity to sign Michael Jordan in the 1984 NBA draft. A week later and the success of Leyton House was splashed across the front pages of the motorsport press. This was no flash in the pan, the

ABOVE: Leyton House's greatest moment – Capelli fends off Alain Prost's Ferrari at the 1990 French Grand Prix.

ABOVE RIGHT: The 1991 season yielded a single point and Leyton House finished 12th in the constructors' table. Here, Mauricio Gugelmin is lapped by Ayrton Senna at the 1991 Italian Grand Prix.

result of a long-shot strategy at Paul Ricard; the improved performance continued over the next few races. Ivan Capelli was running third at Silverstone before his fuel pipe broke, then finished seventh, just outside the points, at Hockenheim. Gugelmin finished eighth in Hungary, then scored a point for sixth in Belgium, finishing just ahead of Capelli who was seventh.

Capelli's six points from France gave him equal tenth in the drivers' championship while the team originally finished seventh in the constructors' title race, but were later promoted to sixth when the Larrousse team were disqualified for declaring the Lola chassis they had used to be their own.

Ian Phillips, who had been supportive of Newey's move to Williams, returned in time for the Hungarian GP, but at the end of the season accepted an offer to join Eddie Jordan's F1 team. The exodus of technical staff continued.

The following season, and now equipped with an Ilmor V10, the March CG911 could only muster one points finish, a sixth place in Hungary, and ended the season just a single point ahead of the teams that needed to pre-qualify. In September 1991, team owner Akira Akagi was implicated in a financial scandal involving his company and the Fuji Bank and was arrested. It was a spectacular decline and fall for a team that had once promised so much.

CONSTRUCTORS' CHAMPIONSHIP POSITIONS

The Manhattan for Adrian Newey's constructors' positions from Leyton House March in 1988 all the way through to Red Bull in 2024. Newey was so close to six-in-a-row with Williams from 1992 to 1997, and many consider that McLaren should have clinched the constructors' title in 1999, were it not for a bargeboard or two ...

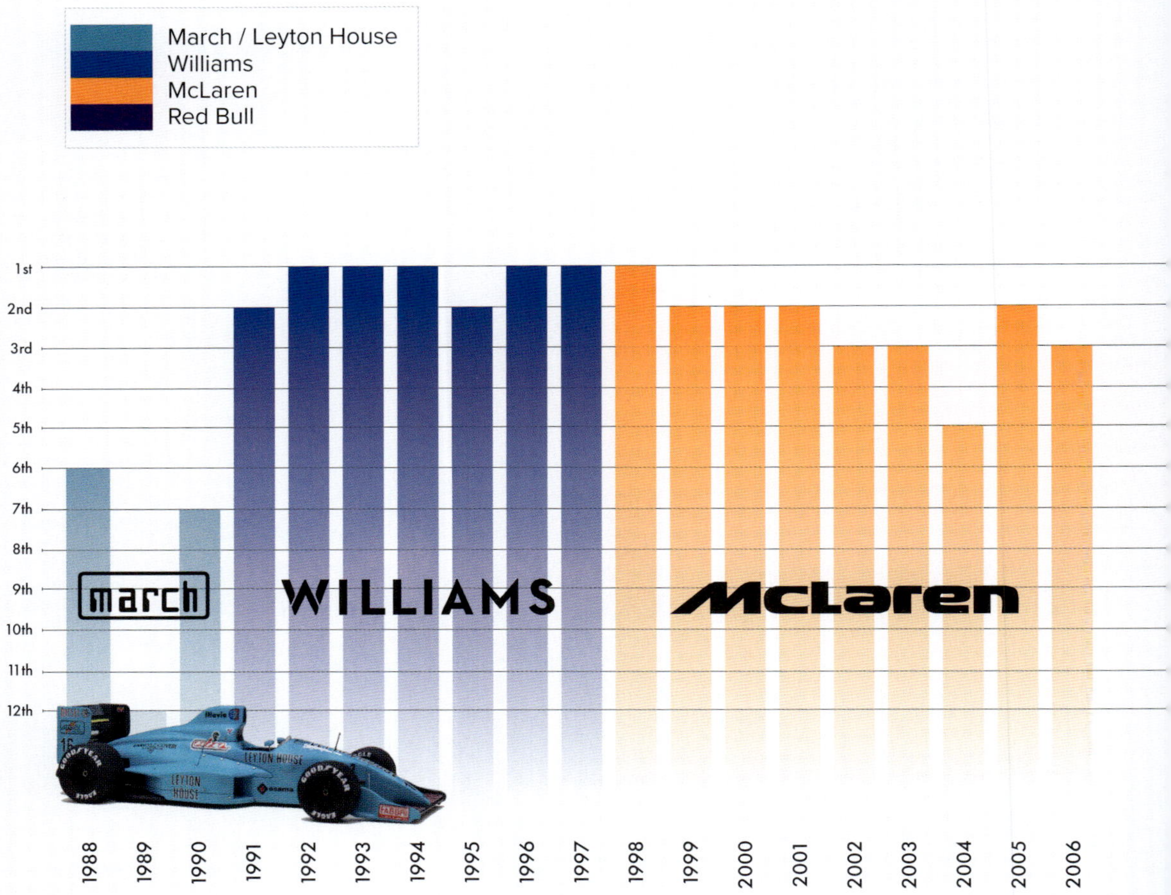

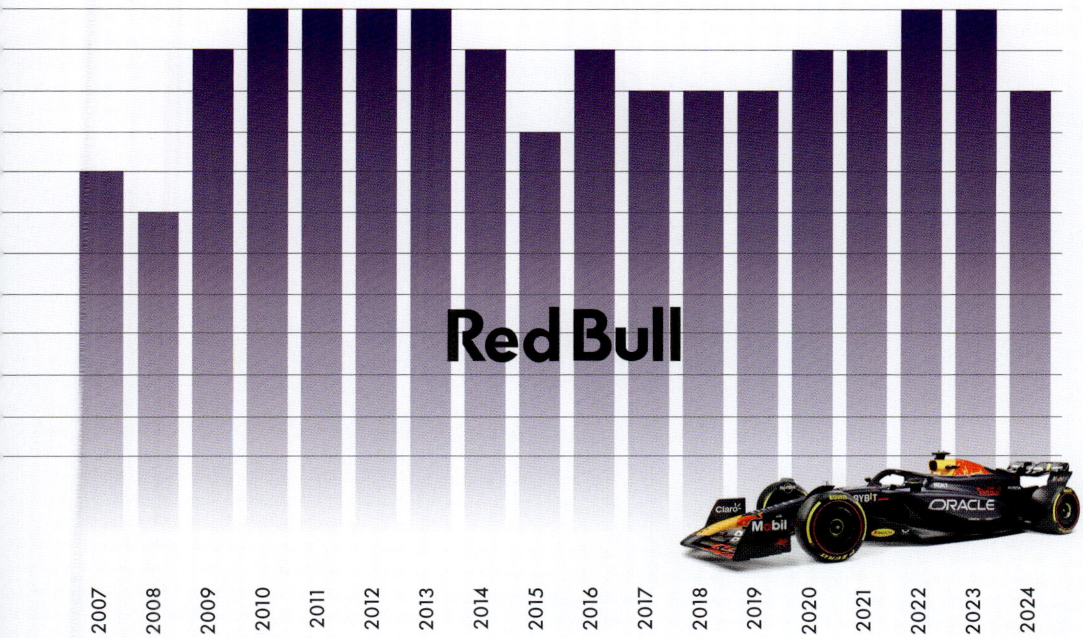
Red Bull
2007
2008
2009
2010
2011
2012
2013
2014
2015
2016
2017
2018
2019
2020
2021
2022
2023
2024

canon
Labatt's
canon
CAMEL
RENAULT
elf
canon
Labatt

4

WILLIAMS

PREVIOUS PAGE: Nigel Mansell 'Red Five' in the 1992 Portuguese Grand Prix at Estoril.

LEFT: Mansell at the wheel of the FW14 in the 1991 Belgian Grand Prix. He qualified third on the grid but retired from the race with an electrical problem.

If central England has a motorsport valley, then Williams Grand Prix Engineering is at the southern end, based south of Oxford. The proximity of so many teams to each other is an enormous benefit, allowing personnel to transfer between teams without massive disruption to their family lives. Adrian's new commute was only 35 minutes, although he was now alone in what had been the family home.

Williams was one of F1's most successful teams, set up by businessman/racing enthusiast Frank Williams, who had been knocking around the F1 paddock for years. It was only after joining forces with lantern-jawed engineer Patrick Head that the team had achieved sustained success. They won their first drivers' World Championship with Alan Jones in 1980, their second in 1982 with Keke Rosberg and their third in 1987 with Nelson Piquet, who 'rewarded' the team for their efforts making him World Champion by taking the team's supply of Honda turbo engines to Lotus in 1988, leaving them stuck with a Judd V8.

Three times the size of the Leyton House team, Newey looked forward to settling into his role of Williams' Head of Research and Development. He would be working for someone (Patrick) with a broad background in race car engineering, who still liked to sketch things on a drawing board and also had a great love of powerful motorbikes. Head would make the annual trip to the French Grand Prix on his beloved BMW. Adrian still had the cachet of producing the March 881, which had been so influential in affecting the direction of travel of Formula 1 design – and in 1988 the smaller team had finished above the 1987 constructors' champions.

LEFT: Mansell and team-mate Riccardo Patrese pose with the team in front of the Williams garage at Circuit de Catalunya in 1991.

RIGHT: The FW14 scored seven wins in the 1991 season, five for Mansell and two for Patrese. Weather conditions were perfect in practice for the final race in Adelaide, but a torrential downpour put an early end to the race on Sunday.

But he was about to be offered a change of job title by Patrick, as he wrote in *How to Build a Car*. 'He called me into his office in order to boom at me. Son of a rear admiral he boomed at everybody, not just me. "I've been impressed with the way your cars went in France and Silverstone," went the boom. (Ivan had led in France and put in the fastest lap at high-speed Silverstone). "I think you should be chief designer, not head of research. Would you prefer that position?"'

Head was confident in the engineering side of the 1990 car, the Williams FW13, but he believed that the aerodynamic side was lacking. Taking up the position in the middle of July, Newey was able to swiftly design a diffuser along the lines of his Leyton House addition and get it on the car for the Hungarian Grand Prix on 12 August. For those who didn't buy into Patrick's theory that the aero side of the Williams-Renault was lacking, the new diffuser gave an increase in performance of about half a second a lap, vindication that the new designer was sorely needed. Williams drivers Thierry Boutsen and Riccardo Patrese locked out the front row of the grid at the Hungaroring. It was Boutsen's only career pole lap and the Belgian driver went on to win the race. Now, Adrian could get on and design the FW14.

Before his departure to Williams he had already started work on what would have been the Leyton House CG911, so he had a firm idea of where he wanted to take the design. Like all F1 transferees he was unable to take any physical designs with him, but there is no copyright in ideas. 'Adrian left it all on the drawing board,' remembers Ian Phillips, 'but the person who took over probably

didn't realise that the car he'd left there turned out to be the 1991 Williams!'

Patrick Head would agree. 'The car had strong heritage, in its visible surfaces, to the Leyton House but was further developed using the wind tunnel at Southampton University.' Even though he now had access to the Williams on-site quarter-scale wind tunnel, Adrian missed the greater accuracy of the 40 per cent tunnel Robin Herd had developed at Comtec. Luckily, Southampton had just bought one from the Ministry of Defence which was 40 per cent and could be run even faster than any of its predecessors.

Without a dramatic change of regulations Newey was keen to evolve his March 901 concept, which he knew to have greater wind tunnel numbers than the FW13. It is a design mantra that he has carried through his career – evolution not revolution. The FW14 followed the same design route as his intended 901 with a

V-shaped chassis and a small cockpit opening, but in 1991 they would not have a driver as small as Ivan Capelli. Nigel Mansell had returned to the team after *Il Leone*'s two years spent at Ferrari and presented a broader, heavier frame to fit in the car, although he was not as tall as the man he was replacing, 6'1" Thierry Boutsen.

Patrick Head designed the gearbox to fit around Newey's design of the aerodynamic elements, the layout of the chassis and suspension. The whole grid had now adopted the John Barnard innovation of a paddle gear-change on the steering wheel, allowing drivers to have two hands on the wheel at all times, and Williams were no different.

Testing brought no clear indication of the 1991 pecking order and in the first two races the team were hampered by gearbox problems. That didn't stop Riccardo Patrese picking up second place in Brazil, but four races into the season the Williams had notched up six retirements with only two finishes – albeit two podium finishes. It seemed that the team were being held back by their Patrick Head-designed gearbox.

The fifth race of the season was in Montreal, producing highlights and lowlights in equal measure. With correct diagnosis the gearbox problem had been solved and the Mansell/Patrese combination locked out the front row of the

BELOW: Mansell picked up a much-celebrated win at Silverstone in 1991 and also a 'racing motorist' who had run out of fuel, on his way back to the pits.

RIGHT: Newey got the chance to work with his fellow Brummie again in 1994 when Nigel deputised in key races during the season.

grid. Adrian was thrilled – his first pole position and his first front row.

It was going to be added to by his first race victory ... or so it seemed. Nigel Mansell drove away from the field from pole and was close to lapping everyone. Such was his lead that he had time to slow down at the hairpin to wave to the fans on the final lap. It has become part of F1 folklore. Failing to change down, his rpm dropped and the engine control unit decided to cut the engine. It was the fatal mistake made by so many athletes, especially professional cyclists, who celebrate the win before crossing the line. The engine revs dropping so low had never happened before, but had Mansell simply driven to the flag and celebrated a lap later, he would have won.

For Newey it was the third time that defeat had been snatched from the jaws of victory – twice at Leyton House and now his first near-miss at Williams. Watching dumbstruck from the Montreal pitwall it would have been hard to convince him that he would go on to score more than 200 race victories in a career lasting close to fifty years. He also didn't have long to wait for success. At the next round in Mexico the Williams duo locked out the front row of the grid again, half a second clear of third-place Senna, and brought the cars home with a 1–2 formation finish.

Patrese fought off a stomach bug and a fast-finishing Nigel Mansell to clinch victory. Mansell then inspired 'Mansell mania' by winning three successive races, in France, Britain and Germany. This included the famous Silverstone slowing-down lap where he picked up Ayrton Senna from the side of the track and drove back to the pits with the World Champion sitting on the FW14's sidepod. Nigel joked that he was tempted to accelerate and lose him through Abbey.

The Williams team pushed McLaren all the way to the end of the season, but with three races to go there was disaster at the Portuguese Grand Prix. At his pit stop, the Williams pit crew sent Mansell off with the right-rear wheel of his car not properly attached. The wheel rotated off, leaving Nigel stranded in the pit lane. Desperate to make up for their mistake, the crew rushed down the pit lane to add the replacement wheel on the spot, as opposed to wheeling it back to the garage and his pit box, as prescribed

by the rules. Mansell was disqualified. At the penultimate race, Japan, the odds were stacked against him and Nigel needed to win the race to keep his championship hopes alive. Gerhard Berger led away and Senna, in second place, did his best to delay the Williams driver, knowing that he had an urgent need to get past. A frustrated Mansell dropped his car into the gravel at Suzuka's Turn 1, the same corner in which Ayrton had expertly taken out his rival Alain Prost the year before. Challenge over.

Williams FW14B

Through 1990 and the summer of 1991 the Williams team had been developing an active ride system, with Damon Hill taking over the development driver role from Mark Blundell. There were huge aerodynamic gains to be made by keeping the car from pitching in high-speed corners, but the drawback was that an active system reduced the driver's feedback through the steering wheel, making it unclear what the car was going to do next.

Naturally, Newey had been investigating active suspension at Leyton House and privately thought that his 'active platform control device' was superior to the Williams approach. The Didcot team had been working with a system first derived from automotive supplier AP Racing, who had given up applying it to road cars and sold the technology to F1.

Both of the team's drivers had their doubts about racing this active suspension mule, the FW14B. Patrick Head put their worries into context in an interview with *Motor Sport* magazine. 'Our active control responded to changes in load distribution, but there was always a small period before the system corrected, and during that period the usual feedback to the driver was not present. There was a fraction of a second delay and it felt to the driver as if he didn't have roll stiffness or roll resistance. Riccardo found that hard to deal with but once Nigel had worked out that, on the other side of this correction, the grip was still there, he learnt to ignore the slightly floaty initial feel of the car.'

Nigel had shown little interest in active ride in his previous stint at Williams, Head revealed, '...and when he came back from Ferrari in 1991 he still wasn't that interested until he heard about the lap times Damon Hill had been achieving in testing. By that time he was more convinced about its safety.'

However, the 1992 car had to be designed through the summer of 1991 while the jury was still out and the test results in the balance. It had been designed as an active ride car with aerodynamics designed to work on a far narrower band of

RIGHT: Adrian Newey with Williams co-owner Patrick Head during the dominant 1992 season.

BELOW: Mansell won the 1992 Mexican Grand Prix from pole. During the season he scored 14 out of 16 pole positions.

ride heights than a passive car. Converting it to a passive car would have been a lot of work. Delays over the final decision pushed the launch of the FW15 back to the start of the European season in 1992. Instead, the team would use the more rigorously tested FW14B for the flyaway races at the start of the year.

As it turned out, such was the advantage of the FW14B that the FW15 was put on hold until 1993. The 1992 car was the most sophisticated piece of racing machinery yet produced, with anti-lock brakes, traction control, launch control, a semi-automatic gearbox and active ride. Apart from problems with the hydraulic

ABOVE: Mansell waves to the crowd after his win at Hockenheim in 1992 – this time, *after* the chequered flag.

pump at Monza which retired Mansell and dropped Patrese from the lead to fifth place, the car was extraordinarily reliable (for the 1990s). It took 15 of 16 poles, ten race wins and Mansell strolled to his first World Championship by the Hungarian Grand Prix in August. In qualifying for the British Grand Prix that summer Mansell was almost two seconds quicker than his team-mate – the kind of gap that would cover 20 cars in Q1 today – and 2.7 and 3.1 seconds quicker than third and fourth on the grid, Messrs Senna and Schumacher, no slouches. It was a crushing display of superiority.

Patrick Head is slightly rueful about the credit for the 1992 car. 'The FW14 and 14B have often been described as Adrian Newey cars but, while he was very much responsible for the outer surfaces, and general architecture, there were a great many other people involved in the design and engineering. Adrian would be the first to accept this.'

Indeed he would – in his autobiography he wrote, 'Of course, most of the credit for the success of the active suspension is down to Patrick. Paddy (Lowe) and Steve (Wise) had got the control side of things working properly; my task was a simple installation job and later to optimise the aerodynamics. The one thing I did from a control point of view was suggest cockpit adjusters, so drivers could fine-tune the system on the go.'

From a personal perspective 1992 was also a good time in his personal life. After his divorce from Amanda he had started dating Marigold, a friend he'd known since his early twenties. They were married in August 1992 (just as Nigel was delivering the first of Adrian's many drivers' titles) with daughters Hannah and Charlotte as bridesmaids. Marigold would soon play an important part in Adrian's career moves – everything at their home at the Old Vicarage, was roses.

Newey once described the Williams team as Frank and Patrick's 'hobby shop'. They were racers who enjoyed racing and kept the business decisions to themselves. It was the antithesis of his previous, struggling team that was solely focused on the bottom line. But one of the decisions that Frank Williams had made in 1991 came to the fore at the latter end of the 1992 season. In 1991 he had signed a contract with Alain Prost (who had taken a sabbatical after being fired from Ferrari in 1991 for calling his car a truck) to drive for them in 1993. One of Prost's alleged conditions in the contract was that he would not be paired with Nigel Mansell again.

WINNING CIRCUITS

Newey is known for producing cars which perform well at circuits with a great deal of medium- to high-speed corners. These are the circuits where he has claimed the most wins, so no surprise that Silverstone, Suzuka and Spa are high on the list.

Silverstone
15 wins
1

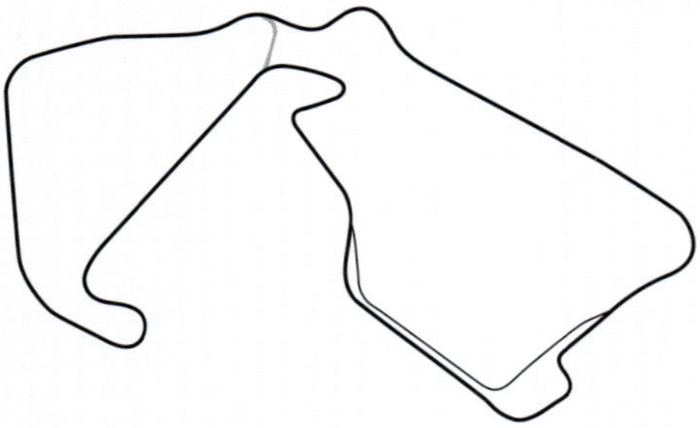

Barcelona
15 wins
=1

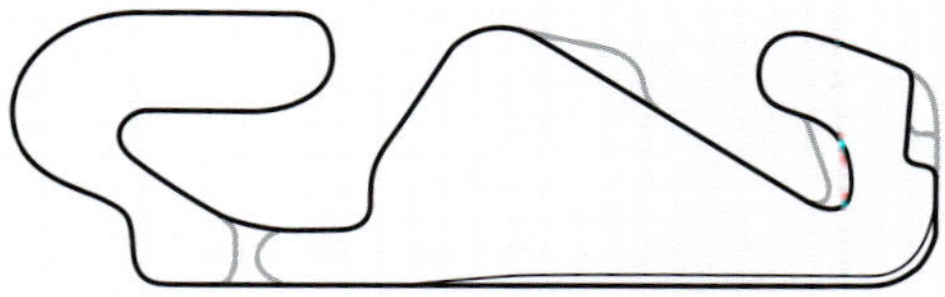

Interlagos
14 wins
3

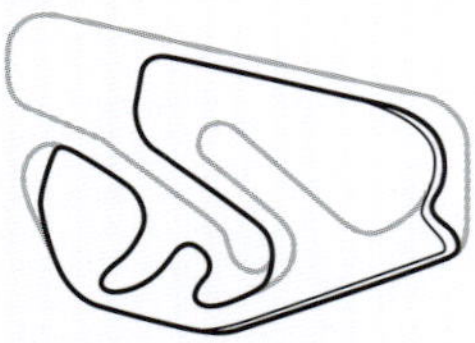

Suzuka
13 wins
4

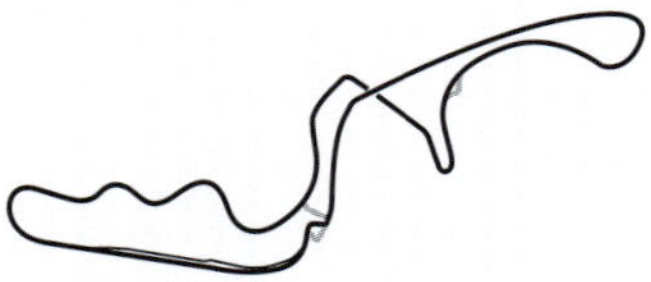

Spa-Francorchamps
12 wins
5

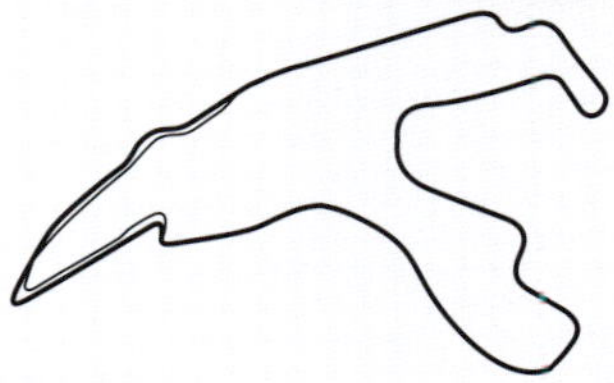

Hungaroring
11 wins
6

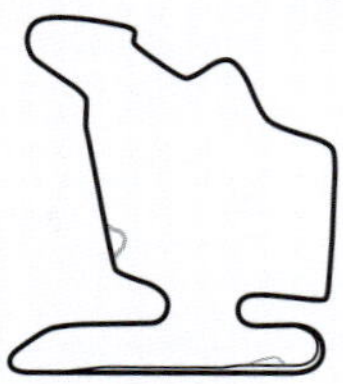

Circuit de Monaco
11 wins
=6

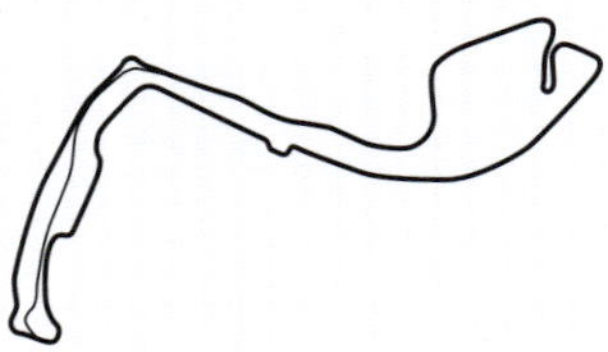

Imola
9 wins
8

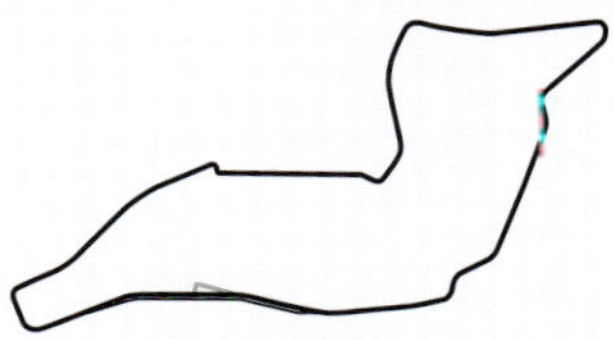

Montreal
9 wins
=8

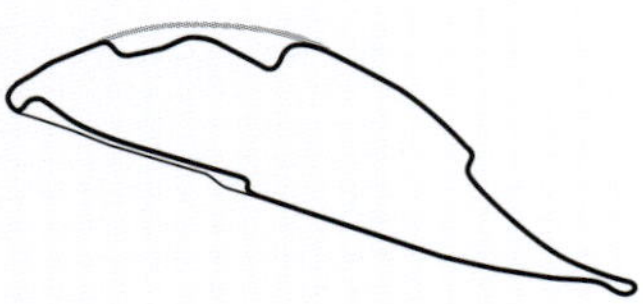

Monza
9 wins
=8

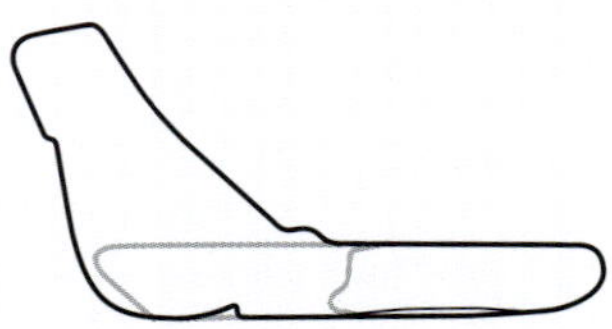

Red Bull Ring
9 wins
=8

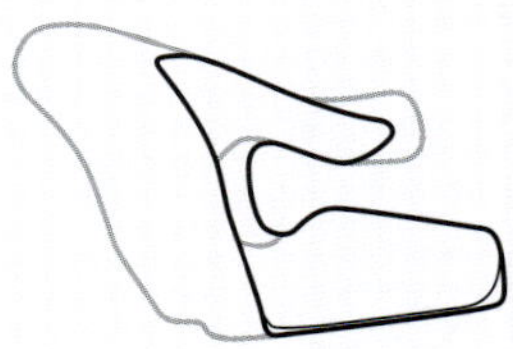

Abu Dhabi **12**
7 wins

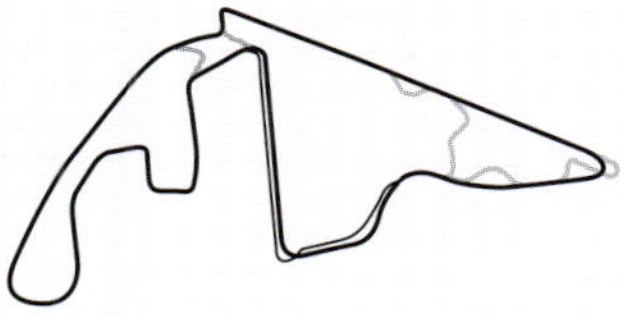

Mexico **=12**
7 wins

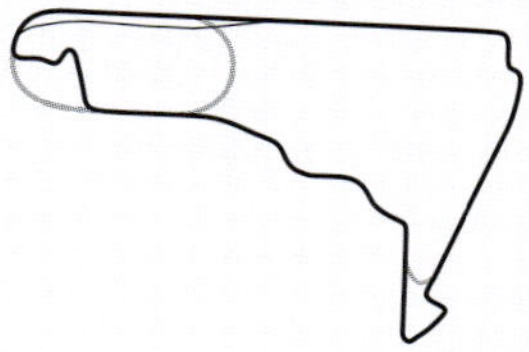

Hockenheim **14**
6 wins

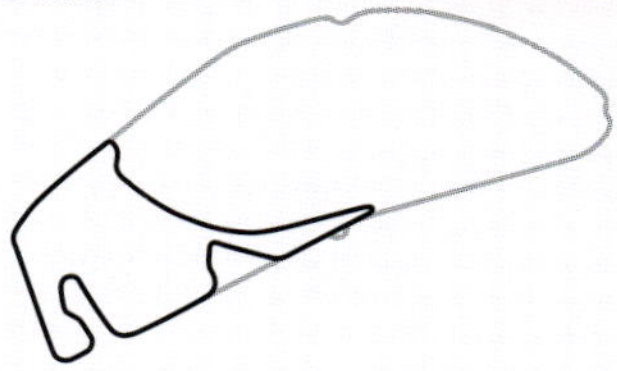

Sepang **=14**
6 wins

Estoril **16**
5 wins

Magny Cours **=16**
5 wins

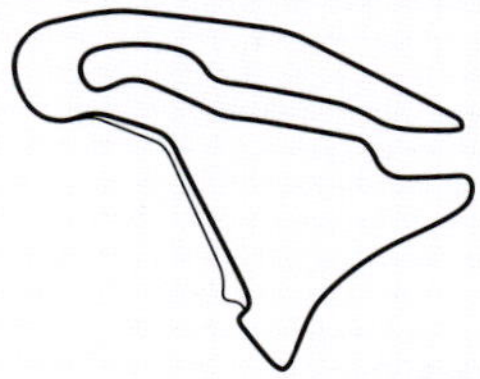

Melbourne **=16**
5 wins

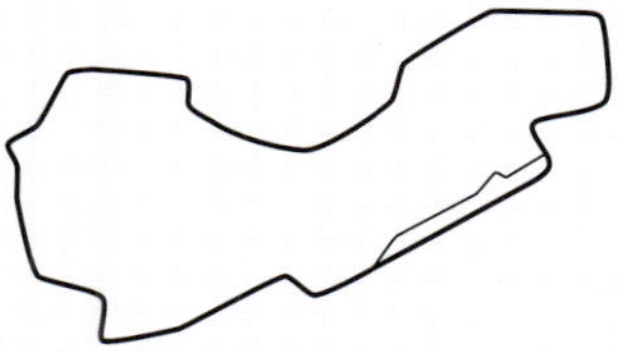

Nürburgring **=16**
5 wins

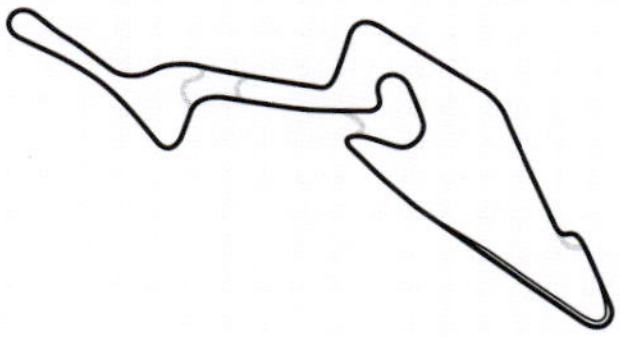

Azerbaijan **=16**
5 wins

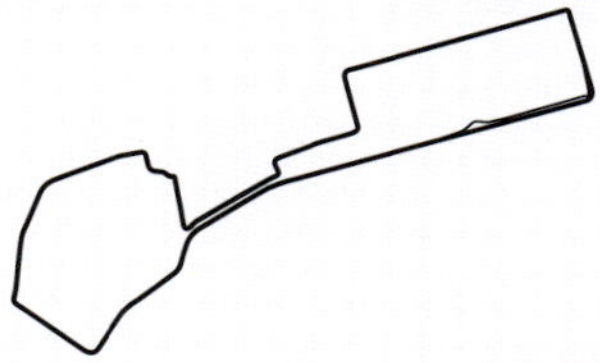

Austin **21**
4 wins

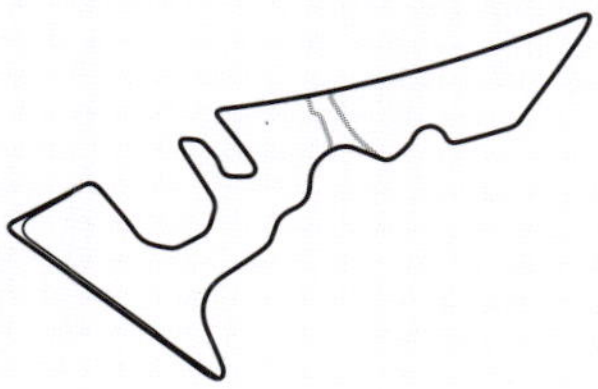

Bahrain **=21**
4 wins

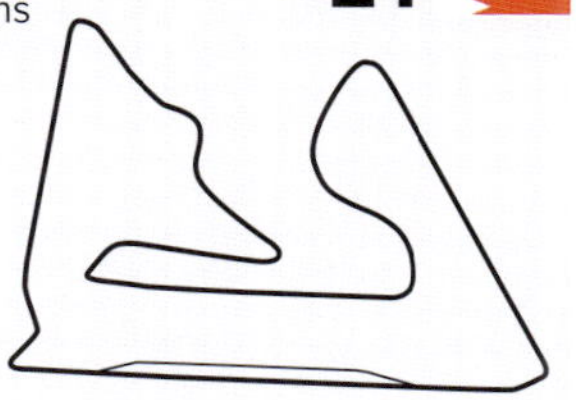

Singapore **=21**
4 wins

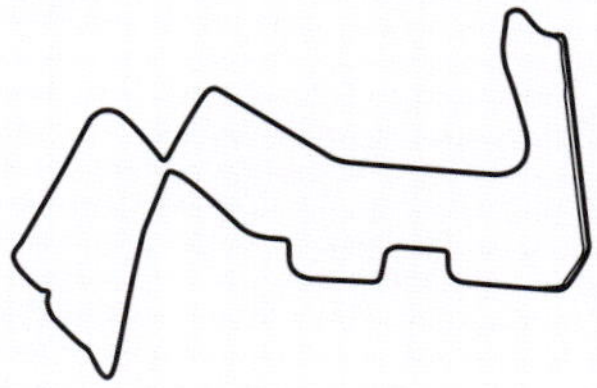

NOTES:

- Newey's cars have claimed wins at 38 circuits
- Only Adrian Newey cars have won the Indian Grand Prix
- His Toro Rosso car won a race before Red Bull did
- Newey has had more wins at Estoril and Sepang than Singapore and Austin
- 223 race wins - 100 by 2005, 200 by 2023, 223 by the end of 2024

* Figures compiled at the close of 2024 season

Prost's valedictory

It is common practice in F1 that the most powerful drivers can predetermine who their team-mates are. Ayrton Senna barred Derek Warwick from joining him at Lotus, Max Verstappen would not contemplate having Carlos Sainz with him when Red Bull ended Sergio Perez's contract early. Prost had not enjoyed his time with Mansell at Ferrari, at one time asking his team boss to secretly switch his chassis with Nigel's as he believed it was quicker. It wasn't and Mansell rumbled it.

When the news came out that the runaway winner of the 1992 World Championship was being ditched by his British team, fans were in uproar. Forget about the tabloid press lionising 'Our Nige', the majority of British Formula 1 fans supported the McLaren and Williams teams and condemnation was universal. Newey also nursed a private unease that his fellow Brummie, the man who had fearlessly chucked the FW14B into high-speed corners and scored 108 points to Patrese's 56 in 1992, was being moved on unnecessarily by the team.

The alternative to Patrese for 1993 was test driver Damon Hill, who had no qualms about active suspension, but who had little F1 race experience – circulating in an underpowered Brabham alongside his test duties in 1992.

The test duties proved key and the press was mollified by the appointment of Damon as Prost's team-mate for 1993. Son of former World Champion Graham

LEFT: Alain Prost, Adrian Newey and race engineer David Brown (right) study a monitor showing qualifying times for the 1993 Canadian Grand Prix.

RIGHT: Alain Prost (2) and Damon Hill (0) finished second and third at the 1993 Portuguese Grand Prix. Hill had qualified on pole, but his engine refused to fire on the parade lap and he had to start from the back of the grid.

– King of Monaco – Hill, Damon was ideally placed for the season ahead, as was the team. Having produced the FW15 nine months before it was due to run in anger, Hill had helped fine-tune the car throughout 1992. It duly swept to championship victory for the team and Prost in 1993. As an indication of Hill's ability to step up and match Prost, he won three races and scored 69 points to Alain's 99. But whereas Damon endured four retirements, Prost's number 2 car – Mansell's removal had meant there was no No.1 – finished every race bar one.

Ayrton Senna

Having restored British fans' faith in the Williams team, Frank then signed Ayrton Senna to drive alongside Prost in 1994 in a pairing that would repeat the incendiary McLaren relationship of 1989. The Brazilian had been so desperate to win again that he had offered to drive for Williams for nothing. Hill would be out. Prost, having manipulated a favourable team-mate for 1993, was not prepared to endure that again and quit, giving Hill a reprieve.

Adrian Newey was fascinated to work with Senna, as he told a *Beyond the Grid* podcast: 'Part of my competitive make-up is that, when you have someone like Ayrton who you're up against and battling year after year, you don't demonise him, but he's the enemy. Of course, I met him occasionally, but never

really talked to him, until he first visited the factory at the end of what must have been 1993.

'I was introduced to him and then straightaway he was asking, "Can I see the wind tunnel models?" So we walked round to the wind tunnel and straightaway he's down on his knees, looking underneath the car, he wanted us to explain what we'd done differently, what was different about this car to the previous car, why we're doing this etc. He was phenomenally inquisitive. You could argue that he didn't need to know that, but for him, he just wanted every bit of information he could possibly have because that might be useful to him at some point in the future. I think probably, more than any other driver I've been involved with [and this includes the equally invested Sebastian Vettel], that's what I found unique about him.'

ABOVE: Ayrton Senna conferring with Newey at the Brazilian Grand Prix in March 1994.

ABOVE LEFT: Alain Prost prepares to start what would turn out to be his final French Grand Prix at Magny Cours in 1993.

LEFT: Damon Hill passing the Benetton of Michael Schumacher during the 1993 French Grand Prix.

Williams had not been alone in devising sophisticated technology for their cars; the second that any F1 team gets a comparative advantage it is seized upon, whether through spy photos, *parc fermé* walk-pasts or even audio analysis of engine output. FIA boss Max Mosley argued that driver skill was being eliminated by traction control, sophisticated anti-lock brakes and active ride. The championship should be a battle of driving not technocrats. And so for 1994 the technology was summarily removed from cars. Of course throughout 1993 teams had been developing cars to suit this technology and the U-turn had tremendous consequences on designs. Compromises suddenly had to be made, especially when it came to enlarging the ride height range.

One of Senna's greatest skills was putting in blindingly fast qualifying laps and, despite doubts that Newey had about the stability of his adapted new car, he managed to put the FW16 on pole for the first three races of the year. At the first race in Brazil he lost the lead to Michael Schumacher thanks to a quicker Benetton fuel stop. After the second round of pit stops he was closing in on Schumacher when, quite uncharacteristically, he spun the car into retirement at the Juncao corner. At the second race, the Pacific GP in Aida, Ayrton Senna was overtaken by Schumacher before the first corner and was then hit from behind by the McLaren of Mika Häkkinen and spun off track. Instead of taking a scooter back to the pits Senna sat at the side of the track listening carefully to the engine note of the Benetton each time it came through. He suspected that, unlike the rest of the field, Schumacher's car was still equipped with traction control. Hence the better start. Hence the ability to lap the entire field at Interlagos.

The next grand prix was at Imola, Italy's second grand prix badged as the San Marino GP. Rubens Barrichello's frightening practice accident on Friday set the tone, with a grave Ayrton visiting his fellow Brazilian in hospital. The mood plunged further on Saturday when a front-wing failure sent the Simtek of Roland Ratzenberger ploughing straight on at the Tosa hairpin, the Austrian killed by the massive deceleration. It was the first death in F1 since Elio de Angelis had been killed testing for the Brabham team at Paul Ricard in 1986, the first grand prix weekend death since 1982. Senna's dark mood deepened and he confided in F1 medic Professor Sid Watkins that he was contemplating not racing.

The race start on Sunday saw more carnage with an unsighted Pedro Lamy piling into the back of JJ Lehto's stalled Benetton on the grid (uncannily, the same type of accident that had killed Riccardo Paletti in 1982). Lamy walked away from the car, but debris scattered the track and flew into the crowd. The cars were recovered while the field, led by Ayrton, circulated behind a shockingly slow Opel Vectra safety car.

BELOW: Damon Hill and Ayrton Senna at the launch of the Williams FW16 in Estoril, January 1994.

RIGHT: Senna in practice for the 1994 San Marino Grand Prix.

It was on the second lap of the re-start that Senna's car hit a bump on the racing line at the fast Tamburello corner and his car suddenly headed for the barrier.

Adrian Newey has huge regrets that he had produced an unstable car for the three-time World Champion. 'I completely messed up the aerodynamics of going back to passive suspension, and the much bigger ride height range that has to cope with. It was a very, very difficult car to drive, and the bumpier the circuit, the worse that became.

'Of course, Imola's quite a bumpy circuit. So what he did with that car was quite extraordinary. In Brazil, he managed to handle it but spun at the last corner near the end of the race. Damon didn't try to extract that level of performance from it and so he finished the race [at Interlagos]. But he knew it was unstable and Ayrton's self-confidence and self-belief in his car control, he would always try it. His concentration was quite extraordinary.'

Although much attention has been devoted to the hastily adapted steering column on the Williams car which investigators believe might have snapped, causing the sudden veering off the circuit, there is a strong likelihood the crash was caused by a slow puncture. There was a question over tyre pressures, having run behind such an ill-suited safety car. 'He did have a big moment on the first lap, but caught it. But on the second lap tyre pressures should have been up, and he should have been fine. The right-rear tyre was destroyed. So we will never know,' he told Jake Humphrey. 'What I do know is the car was aerodynamically unstable, the diffuser was stalling at very low ride height, and Ayrton, having lost the first two races, was absolutely determined to carry the car and win that race. And so that's the responsibility I have to live with.

'Stupid as it sounds, I've never, ever thought or questioned, if somebody gets badly hurt or worse in a car that I've been overall responsible for, how am I going to feel? And when it happened, it was ... I mean the biggest memory of those

bloody klaxons, when all the noise all the spectators made with all these images of Ayrton sitting upright in the car, you're hoping desperately he's okay.

'"What a waste" was the biggest, single emotion, what a waste of such an amazing person, such a stupid accident, and such an unlucky accident. If it hadn't been for the wishbone leg [striking Ayrton's helmet] then he would have been absolutely unhurt. But of course, in the aftermath, you go through the initial emotion of, "Do I want to continue working in motor racing?"

'There'd be something wrong with you if you didn't question yourself and what you're doing. First of all, it would have been quite selfish because if Patrick or I, or both of us, had decided we were stopping, we would have left the team in complete disarray.

'And at the same time, Patrick and I were both charged with manslaughter, which lasted for about ten years, which was a pressure, because it wasn't the key thing for me, the key thing was, what part did I personally play in what happened? And I don't think we'll ever know with absolute, 100 per cent confidence what happened, none of the data points to the steering column being a problem. What the data does show is that the car snaps sideways in a corner that should have been flat.'

Damon Hill

Newey was impressed with the grit that Damon showed in response to his team-mate's fatal accident. 'Of course, Damon was in the exact same position as his dad had been in when Jim Clark passed [at Hockenheim in an F2 race]. But it was much more extreme for Damon because he was still only in his second proper season in Formula 1 and was now the team leader. I think his inner strength and mettle to then carry things forwards from there was quite extraordinary. He had to carry the team forward and the fact that he did that and took it down to the wire in 1994, I think was phenomenal.'

ABOVE: Senna leads into the Tosa hairpin at Imola in 1994 pursued by Schumacher, Berger and Damon Hill. The Brazilian was fighting a massively unstable car.

LEFT: Senna gets a good start from pole at the 1994 San Marino Grand Prix, but further back the stalled JJ Lehto is about to be collected by Pedro Lamy's Lotus.

The 1994 season was a scrappy affair with the Benetton of Flavio Briatore/Ross Brawn/Pat Symonds subject to multiple legal queries. At the German Grand Prix in Hockenheim it was discovered the team had illegally speeded up their fuel stops by removing a filter out of the standard FIA-approved apparatus. When it failed to close properly the fuel spillage produced a pit lane inferno of terrifying proportions which could have ended the career – or life – of Jos Verstappen in the second car. Considering it was a proven deliberate act of removal that could have resulted in the season's third fatality, there was great surprise when the Benetton team went unpunished.

The illegal traction control was investigated. Despite delaying tactics from Benetton, and other rival teams across the grid, investigators eventually found Launch Control as Option 13 – carefully obscured in the software, but still available. The FIA failed to take any action against Benetton who argued it was an immense software task to remove it and so had left it there, *unused*. The argument was wholly inaccurate. Patrick Head noted that Williams' own traction control (for 1992) was 'one of the easiest and most rapidly supplied 0.5-0.7seconds gains in speed that has ever been applied to a racing car. Paddy Lowe joked that it took him about 15 minutes to write the code for the first system. Not quite the case, but close.'

Added to that, Michael Schumacher indulged in a questionable driving style that saw him banned from some races. In the latter stages of the season the German would take to the motorsport press to taunt Damon Hill. It all came down to the final race in Adelaide, with Schumacher still leading the championship by a single point. Leading the race but under pressure from a closing Damon Hill he had driven off track, colliding with the barriers, seriously damaging his car. An unsighted Hill came upon the slow-moving car and decided it was now or never. Schumacher saw him coming in his mirrors and turned into the Williams.

Adrian Newey was watching the world TV pictures back in England hard at work on the FW17. He was powerless to intervene. Schumacher was out on the spot, but Damon was able to limp back to the pits with a bent left-front suspension where he was told to retire the car. Given the gaps in the field, he would only have needed to finish fifth to take the drivers' title (fifth-place Olivier Panis finished a lap down). He might have been able to coast round, taking it easy at the four left-hand corners had Newey been able to intervene with advice. As it was, Damon cut a dignified figure in defeat. Williams took their third successive constructors' championship, but there was little joy from a season overshadowed by tragedy and a manslaughter charge in Italy that would drag on for years.

BELOW: David Coulthard in the No.6 Williams receives a punt up the inside from the Ferrari of Jean Alesi at the start of the 1995 Monaco Grand Prix. Alesi then clunked into Ferrari team-mate Gerhard Berger and the race was red-flagged.

The 1995 driver dilemma

In 1995, the Benetton team got themselves a more powerful engine and although Newey believed Williams had 'on balance' the quicker car, a series of high-profile accidents and poor reliability cost them dear. The qualifying record of the FW17 was good. Between them Damon Hill and David Coulthard racked up 12 pole positions for the 17 races, but they were outraced by Michael Schumacher, now partnered by Johnny Herbert.

At Silverstone Hill tried an overambitious overtaking move on Schumacher and took them both out, gifting a hugely popular win for Johnny Herbert. In Adelaide, Coulthard suffered the embarrassment of a crash in the pit lane while leading the Australian Grand Prix.

There were further shenanigans with Benetton. In the week leading up to the British GP, Newey reignited the controversy over the similarities between the Benetton B195 and the Ligier JS41 chassis. It had become apparent at the opening race in Brazil that the Ligier was a copy of the B195 – effectively either IP theft or a customer car. They had different engines installed but were otherwise the same – Ligier was part-owned by Benetton boss Flavio Briatore. Despite an

FIA investigation that declared the JS41 legal earlier in the season, Newey was adamant that, 'as far as suspension geometry and aerodynamics are concerned, I'd say they are identical ... taken to a logical conclusion, we'll be in an IndyCar position [customer cars]. It is very dangerous.' Frank Williams once told Adrian he was the most competitive person he knew, which took the designer aback, but here was another manifestation.

The 1995 season might have seen a loss of Williams' constructors' crown, but from a career perspective, interest in Newey's employment had never been greater. His Williams contract was up for renewal and Maranello beckoned. He had first gone for interview there when Ferrari were considering an IndyCar project and were on the scout for a chief designer. The project never came to be, but in 1995 new boss Jean Todt was assembling a team to bring back a driver's

title that had eluded the Scuderia since 1979. Newey was tempted to step in to try and succeed where ex-McLaren designer John Barnard had failed. However, his time at Truesports in Ohio with first wife Amanda made him wary.

He was now a father for the third time with new daughter Imogen and, though wife Marigold was happy to transfer to Emilia-Romagna, moving abroad would restrict time with daughters Charlotte and Hannah.

He was also offered the job as technical director by McLaren's Martin Whitmarsh. So, two of the prime jobs in F1 could be his. What he wanted from a new Williams contract was more money and to be involved in the policy-making of the team. He wanted to be consulted on engine choice and particularly driver choice, after the sacking of Nigel Mansell had come as an ugly surprise. The 'hobby shop' decision circle had to be expanded. With those reassurances in place, Adrian signed a new three-year contract in June 1995.

Soon afterwards David Coulthard announced he would be leaving to join McLaren the following year, so a driver vacancy arose alongside Damon Hill for 1996. Craig Pollock, Jacques Villeneuve's manager, got in touch with the team. Gilles Villenueve's son was on his way to winning the 1995 CART IndyCar championship and was looking to swap open-wheel series. Frank and Patrick agreed to a Silverstone test. As it was scheduled for the time Adrian would be away on a family holiday in Barbados they agreed that if Jacques could get within a second of a benchmark time set by Damon, then it would be worth a second test. In the end he was close to two seconds slower ... and was signed.

Newey arrived back from his vacation to find that the old lunchtime decisions over a fine bottle of wine were still in place. He reminded them of their agreement and Frank apologised, assuring his chief designer it wouldn't happen again.

LEFT: Damon Hill on his way to victory at the 1996 French Grand Prix at Magny Cours, one of eight wins in his World Championship season.

BELOW: Adrian Newey stepped in as race engineer for Damon Hill during the 1996 season.

BELOW RIGHT: Rookie Jacques Villeneuve took four wins and 11 podiums in an impressive debut season.

Adventures in high rake

The FW18 of 1996 was the first of what would typify Newey designs stretching into the Red Bull era, a high-rake car, low at the front, high at the back. There were advantages and disadvantages to this approach, but even the crude simulation tools Williams employed suggested this was the route to go.

Adrian had also spotted his favourite thing, a loophole in the minimum chassis height regulations that (it soon transpired) all the other teams had failed to appreciate. It gave them an advantage not easily duplicated across the course of the season. At the first race in Melbourne the FW18s locked out the front row with Jacques Villeneuve on pole. Barring the first ever F1 grand prix in 1950, the fairytale start of a rookie winning his first race had only been accomplished once, by Ferrari's Giancarlo Baghetti. Villeneuve looked to replicate the feat, leading for the majority of the race until an oil leak slowed him, allowing Damon Hill to close

in and take victory ahead of the Canadian.

Damon won four of the first five races, with Jacques often in close attendance. Very soon it became clear that the 1996 season was going to be a battle between the two Williams drivers and – with none of the team orders that would blight F1 in the Schumacher/Ferrari era – the duo were free to race. Adrian was distinctly biased towards Damon, and not because he had once constructed a model of his father's Lotus 49B. To fill a gap in experience in the race team he had moved back into race engineering on Damon's side of the garage, his first return to the role for almost a decade.

ABOVE: Damon celebrates after winning the final race in Japan in 1996.

RIGHT: Jacques Villeneuve closes in on Michael Schumacher's Ferrari in the season-defining final race in Jerez, 1997. Villeneuve's third place in the Williams FW19 put another two world titles on the Newey CV.

Williams wrapped up the constructors' title by the Hungarian Grand Prix, but heading into the final race, the Japanese GP, Damon led by nine points and needed just a single point to clinch the drivers' title. Villeneuve had grabbed pole at Suzuka with Damon alongside him on the front row. It all changed when the lights went out. Jacques made a poor start and fell to sixth while Damon took a lead he would not relinquish, converting it to his eighth win of the season.

'And Damon Hill exits the chicane and wins the Japanese Grand Prix – and I've got to stop, because I've got a lump in my throat!' yelled Murray Walker in his iconic BBC commentary and most of the listening public were with him on that. Murray had commentated on Graham Hill winning in the 1960s and now here was the first son of a World Champion becoming World Champion.

It was a bittersweet moment. Earlier that year, on a flight back from the Belgian Grand Prix, Patrick Head confirmed rumours that had been emerging since the German GP that Sauber driver Heinz-Harald Frentzen had been signed to the team for 1997. Patrick explained to a quietly seething Adrian that Damon had driven badly in 1995, so they had looked around for emerging talent. Frentzen had scored a solitary podium in 1995 and managed three points finishes in 1996 ... it had happened again. Frank and Patrick had hired a driver without consulting him, also ejecting a popular British driver directly after he had won a drivers' title.

Newey went straight to Frank Williams to have the truth confirmed and told him that yet again he had overridden their agreement. Except now he would be 'reviewing his options'. Patrick Head was having none of it, blustering that he had a three-year contract to fulfil. Frank wanted to offer him more money to stay – he had already completed most of the 1997 car – but it was too late. Once the news emerged, McLaren's Martin Whitmarsh had immediately been on the phone to enquire of Newey's availability.

'I liked Martin Whitmarsh, I liked the set-up, I liked the fact that if I joined them I'd be working with DC again,' he wrote in *How to Build a Car*. 'I liked the fact that they were using a Mercedes engine designed and manufactured by my old friend (from IndyCar days) Mario Illien at Ilmor Engines in Brixworth.' It was time to move on.

Davi
Sun
Computer

5

McLAREN

While his Williams FW19 was winning the 1997 World Championship for Jacques Villeneuve and, significantly, not Heinz-Harald Frentzen, Adrian was stuck in litigation. He had left Williams on 7 November, 1996 and would not start work for McLaren until 1 August, 1997. Apart from dealing with a Williams injunction intended to have him on gardening leave until 1998, the Senna manslaughter charges had to be dealt with.

Newey revealed a sensitive side that may have foreshadowed his unexpected departure from Red Bull many years later. 'At McLaren the buck would stop with me. I wanted to show that I didn't need Patrick to calm my so-called "excesses",' he wrote in his autobiography. 'There had sprung up an enduring paddock myth that I somehow needed "reining in" and that during my time at Williams, Patrick stopped me going too far. I didn't feel it was true ... I wanted to show that I was capable of leading the entire engineering side of the company without somebody effectively editing my work.'

Nine months is a long time to be 'gardening', so Adrian had time to do some initial concepts before he arrived at the Woking HQ. His arrival would coincide with another FIA bid to slow down cars with a change of the regulations for 1998. Cars would now be slimmed down from 2m to 1.8m wide and tyres would have grooves to reduce the contact patch of rubber on tarmac.

The McLaren MP4/13 would start taking shape at home. 'I didn't have any data to back up my initial thoughts – because I was working from my bedroom,' he told *Motor Sport*'s Mark Hughes, 'but I felt that lowering the centre of gravity would become crucial because the narrow track would bring more weight transfer and the grooved tyres would be less consistent as the grip co-efficient would fall away more as loads went up.

'I started working with Mario Illien at Ilmor in secret, to get the crankshaft height down because that not only lowers the whole engine but also the gearbox internals. A low seating position obviously became important because if you could get the driver's upper body lower, then you could lower the surrounding structure, the roll hoop etc. Then visibility becomes a problem.

PREVIOUS PAGE: David Coulthard rides the kerbs during practice for the 2004 Canadian Grand Prix, a no-tobacco-sponsorship race, and hence his name plastered over the rear wing.

RIGHT: Mika Häkkinen and David Coulthard pose in front of the new McLaren MP4/13 in its testing livery, the now very familiar papaya orange.

'One of the guys working at McLaren when I started there had spotted that although the drawing [in the regulations] showed a rectangular box, it actually said 'depth'. It didn't say it had to be a rectangle.' Effectively they could make a very shallow chassis in height then put a couple of fins up the side to legalise it ...
'We started working with David Coulthard and it was DC who said, "My vision is binary; I'm either looking straight ahead for the braking area or I'm looking diagonally across at the apex." So we could put these fins in the bits in between

without really bothering the driver. That's what led to the MP4/13 chassis which was a good step.'

The late 'official' start meant it would be a very compressed design cycle, but McLaren had the experience and expertise to move quickly. Newey also extended the wheelbase to maintain corner entry stability. 'That was a unique feature of that 1998 car. Unfortunately, Ross Brawn at Ferrari spotted it and they started to move their front axle forwards. But we were first on that one and it wasn't the only feature. We managed to get the car very light, very low centre of gravity, to try and minimise the weight transfer onto these very fragile tyres.'

Adrian had arrived in Woking on the first day of August with many technical drawings all dated, for legal reasons, 1 August. The team were yet to move to the Norman Foster-designed McLaren Technology Centre, but the overriding colour scheme of the factory was still universal, Ron Dennis-inspired grey. Except, that is, for John Barnard's former design office, which resembled the saloon of the Mary

BELOW: Coulthard leads the Ferrari of Schumacher with its ugly winglets (that Tyrrell first ran in 1997), and team-mate Mika Häkkinen in the 1998 San Marino Grand Prix at Imola. Winglets were banned by the Spanish GP.

BELOW RIGHT: Mika Häkkinen collides with the Sauber of Johnny Herbert after the second start of the chaotic 1998 Belgian Grand Prix.

Celeste, all mahogany panelling and hardly touched since Barnard had left to design for Ferrari at the end of the 1980s.

The Newey family had moved from Fyfield in Oxfordshire to a house in Ascot, Berkshire, to cut the commute and were knee-deep in paint charts for the new house. Adrian immediately commissioned the factory manager to transform this 'cheerless' space with a duck-egg blue paint scheme. When McLaren boss Ron Dennis saw the transformation he was aghast, but chose to say nothing to his new design chief.

Although early wind tunnel results showed that the 'Newey bedroom MP4/13' was slower than the factory-designed test model, Cypriot aerodynamicist Peter Prodromou thought it showed promise. Prodroomu would go on to follow Newey to Red Bull in 2006.

Gradually, performance was added to the car as Adrian worked maximum hours to get the 1998 car faster. He had enjoyed strong early success with March

and Williams and didn't want his first season with the men in grey to be anything less. At a private test at Paul Ricard the carbon composite rear top wishbone had broken. McLaren hurriedly produced a steel substitute but that meant missing the first two official test days at Barcelona. It was less than optimal.

ABOVE: Mika Häkkinen turns into Rascasse at the 1998 Monaco Grand Prix, which he won from pole.

The Newey Effect

Then, on the third day of the four-day test, Mika Häkkinen went over a second quicker than anybody else. The MP4/13 topped the timesheets at the second four-day test as well. The omens were good, but Newey was well aware that in testing one can never be sure of others' fuel loads and engine settings – and rival teams seldom brought along innovative aero elements that could easily be copied.

The cars were shipped off to Melbourne and, much to his relief, the McLarens locked out the front row of the grid with Mika on pole and David 0.7 seconds clear of Michael Schumacher in third. The race unfolded to plan with Mika leading into the first corner and the McLarens on course for a resounding 1–2, lapping the entire field. But Mika's hearing had never been the best after a life-threatening 1995 crash in Adelaide where a punctured tyre had sent him into the barriers at Brewery Bend. He misheard a radio call to be careful on the brakes and came into the pits, only to be waved straight through by the team. Except now he was behind DC. Ron Dennis got on the radio and asked him to let Mika back through, indeed there had been a pre-race agreement that whoever got to the first corner in the lead would take the win if they were line astern.

It caused a minor furore over team orders and cries of 'race manipulation', but nothing like the collective paddock angst over McLaren's 'brake steer' pedal. This was a system they had been running since 1997, where a fourth pedal was used to help lock the inside-rear brake going into a corner to help turn-in. It was entirely legal and passed by the FIA's Charlie Whiting, but had been exposed in *F1 Racing* magazine when photographer Darren Heath had managed to get his camera inside the cockpit of an MP4/12 that had broken down and been abandoned by DC at the side of the track. Heath also managed to get photos of the McLaren with one glowing rear brake disc and one showing no heat at all.

The following race was the Brazilian Grand Prix and the absence of the now-banned brake steer – 'because Ferrari tried it and couldn't get it to work' – did nothing to dent the McLaren dominance. At Interlagos it was another 1–2 with pole and fastest lap. It was also good news for tyre supplier Bridgestone, their first two GP wins, having joined the grid a year earlier.

As the season progressed it was shaping up to be a battle between the Ferrari of Michael Schumacher and the McLaren of Mika Häkkinen. One race that Adrian was desperate to win was around the streets of Monte Carlo. In 1992 and 1996 when the Williams had been dominant, events conspired to lose him F1's blue riband race. Qualifying in Monaco is everything and in 1998, Häkkinen put the McLaren on pole, with the added insurance of DC as rear gunner in P2. To ensure that Mika's natural exuberance didn't get the better of him, Adrian had reinforced the suspension of the Finn's car in case he sustained contact with the wall.

In the race, Coulthard disappeared from the lapcharts with engine problems on Lap 17, but Häkkinen clinched victory by 11 seconds. Better still, Schumacher finished two laps down and out of the points. Adrian had celebrated a tenth place for Ivan Capelli at the 1988 Monaco Grand Prix by riding a hire scooter into the harbour. This time round, dressed in the corporate grey of McLaren, he stuck to the champagne.

Advantage in the battle between Ferrari and McLaren swung back and forth in 1998. Rain, as ever, had come to the Belgian Grand Prix. It was a race that saw the biggest multi-car pile-up in the sport since 1973 after the McLaren of David Coulthard twitched into the Ferrari of Eddie Irvine following the exit from La Source hairpin. Cars pinballed across the track from barrier to barrier, causing an immediate red flag. The 1973 Jody Scheckter-led pile-up at Silverstone's Woodcote corner eliminated 11 cars and had been witnessed by Adrian and his father, attending their first F1 grand prix.

Luckily F1 had yet to ban spare cars in 1998, so an hour later the re-assembled grid was lacking just four drivers. At the re-start Häkkinen lost control at La Source and was hit by Johnny Herbert's Sauber, sending Mika into retirement. A further tangle with Alex Wurz had dropped Coulthard to the back of the field and on Lap 25, when Schumacher came up to lap him in heavy rain, the Scot lifted off to let him past, though staying on the dry-ish inside line. Schumacher clattered into the back of the McLaren, converting his car to a three-wheeler and immediate retirement. Having pitted he stormed down the pit lane to have it out with DC in a rare display of F1 'handbags'. The stewards saw nothing wrong after a post-race protest. Michael then turned his ire towards Eddie Jordan, who had not wished his drivers to throw away a first-ever Jordan team victory by racing each other and asked Ralf Schumacher to hold station behind winner Damon Hill. An irate Schumi Sr then bought his younger brother's contract off EJ for an alleged £2m.

At the following race in Monza, Häkkinen looked set up for victory when a brake problem he had been managing for most of the race allowed his German rival past – he cascaded down the order to finish fourth. With two races to go, the drivers were now level on points. At the penultimate race, the Luxembourg Grand Prix, Mika displayed a masterclass of Finnish cool by passing the road-blocking Eddie Irvine and then used the overcut to pass Schumacher at the first pit stops. Thus the McLaren team arrived at the final race in Suzuka leading the drivers' championship by four points. All Mika needed was to finish second, even if Schumi won.

As it turned out, Michael made his job a lot easier. Starting from pole, with Mika alongside him, the German stalled on the formation lap and was forced to catch up the rest of the cars and start from the back of the grid. He stormed

ADRIAN NEWEY AT MONACO

A win at Monaco always eluded Adrian at Williams, despite the world titles, but he has more than made up for that with Red Bull. The results shown are the best result for the team that year.

RETIRED:
1990 March CG901
1994 Williams FW16
1996 Williams FW18
1997 Williams FW19
2004 McLaren MP4-19
2020 No race

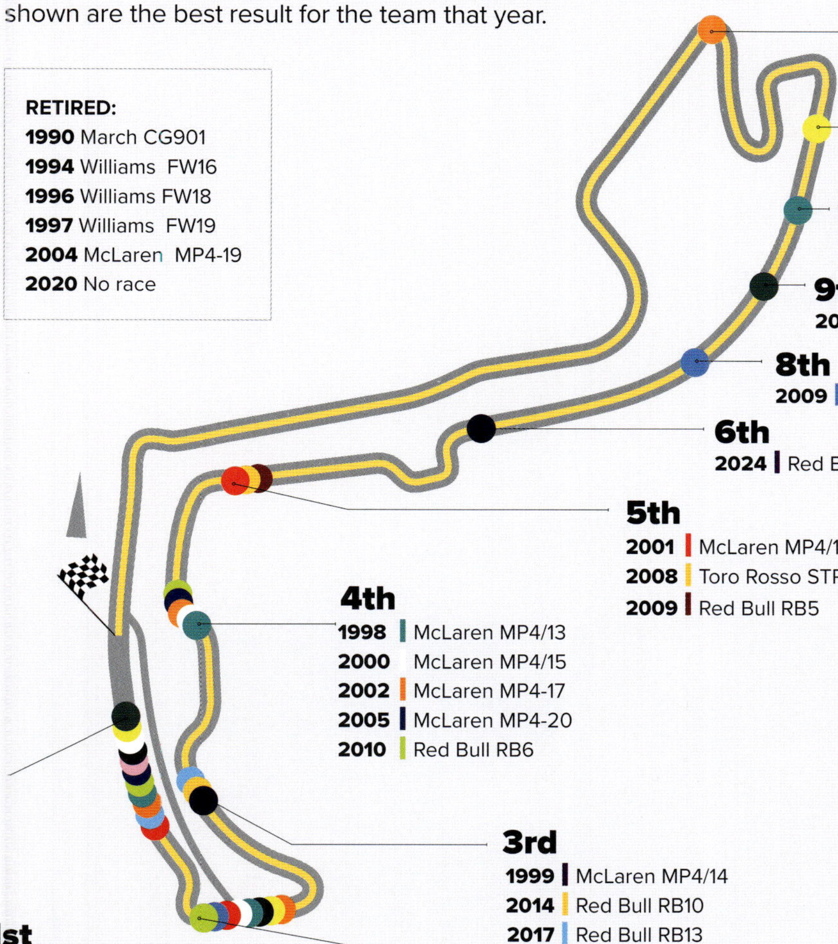

14th
2007 Red Bull RB3

11th
1989 March CG891

10th
1988 March 881

9th
2007 Toro Rosso STR2

8th
2009 Toro Rosso STR4

6th
2024 Red Bull RB20

5th
2001 McLaren MP4/14
2008 Toro Rosso STR3
2009 Red Bull RB5

4th
1998 McLaren MP4/13
2000 McLaren MP4/15
2002 McLaren MP4-17
2005 McLaren MP4-20
2010 Red Bull RB6

3rd
1999 McLaren MP4/14
2014 Red Bull RB10
2017 Red Bull RB13

1st
1998 McLaren MP4/13
2000 McLaren MP4/15
2002 McLaren MP4-17
2005 McLaren MP4-20
2010 Red Bull RB6
2011 Red Bull RB7
2012 Red Bull RB8
2018 Red Bull RB14
2021 Red Bull RB17
2022 Red Bull RB18
2023 Red Bull RB19

2nd
1991 Williams FW14
1992 Williams FW14B
1993 Williams FW15C
1995 Williams FW17
2003 McLaren MP4-17D
2006 McLaren MP4-21
2013 Red Bull RB9
2016 Red Bull RB12

through the field, but a win looked unlikely – and then a puncture on Lap 31 ended any slim hope he might catch the Flying Finn. Mika took the race win.

Newey had won his sixth constructors' championship and his fifth drivers' title – what's more, he had delivered the titles with his first car for McLaren. Even better, perhaps, he had become father to son Harrison, his fourth child born in July 1998, and surely that would mean becoming a karting dad somewhere down the line ...

1999: To the wire

There were no rule changes for the following season, so Adrian could do what he does best – evolve the previous year's model. And given that he had created the MP4/13 in haste after signing on in August, he had the positive luxury of testing the MP4/14 from May 1998.

All looked well when the F1 paddock reconvened in Albert Park for the Australian Grand Prix – there were the two McLarens on the front row – and this year Mika was a mighty 1.3 seconds ahead of third-place Michael in qualifying. The race proved quite different. By the 21st lap the mechanics were packing up the cars to be freighted to Brazil, both out with technical issues.

Over the course of the year McLaren would rack up 12 retirements between the two drivers compared to four for their nearest rival, Ferrari. Exiting the French Grand Prix Mika Häkkinen was leading the championship by eight points from Schumacher and 14 points from Irvine.

The season was turned on its head at Silverstone. Eddie Irvine got away in front of his Ferrari team-mate at the start and pounding down the Hangar straight Schumacher looked like he wanted to get past the Ulsterman in a hurry. After a puff of smoke at the braking point for Stowe corner, his car continued on across the gravel unabated and hit the tyre barriers head on. Its brakes had failed. Schumacher was carefully extracted from the car, but had sustained a broken leg that would sideline him for all but two further races in the season.

BELOW LEFT: Adrian was on the podium for the fifth race of the 1999 season, the Spanish Grand Prix.

BELOW: A good view of the rear diffuser on the MP4/14.

There were reasons to be cheerful, though. It helped give McLaren their first British Grand Prix victory in ten years. The podium places of Coulthard and Irvine (first and second) also marked the last time two British drivers would stand together on the podium at their home event until the 2023 British GP where Lando Norris and Lewis Hamilton finished second and third.

Ferrari drafted in strong midfield runner Mika Salo as Irvine's new team-mate and the Finn dutifully handed over the chance of his only ever F1 race win at Hockenheim, the Ferraris finishing 1–2. Irv gave him the trophy but kept the points, while McLaren were left with another DNF for Häkkinen after a tyre failure.

With two races to go Häkkinen led Irvine by only two points, thanks in part to the 'lack of focus' from the McLaren team, along with Ferrari's relentless development of their car. In the days of no budget cap, money could be thrown at the car – and some of those euros went into creating new barge boards for the F399. Schumacher returned for the penultimate race in Malaysia and duly handed over the race win to Irvine, while Häkkinen came home third. It was now advantage Irvine who would be four points ahead going into the final race in Japan. Until the race stewards intervened ...

In *parc fermé* after the race Adrian spotted that the new Ferrari barge boards looked like they didn't have a big enough shadow plate to cover them, i.e. they had been manufactured too big for the plate below. The FIA's technical director Charlie Whiting went down to take a look and agreed with Newey's assessment. Ferrari were excluded from the results. 'Ross Brawn, then in charge of engineering at Ferrari, in a surprising moment of frankness admitted to the media that the boards did indeed exceed the maximum permitted dimension,' wrote FIA boss Max Mosley in his autobiography. 'The boards were impounded and brought back to FIA headquarters pending the inevitable appeal.' Though why Max thought it would be *inevitable* if the Ferrari team technical director had admitted they were illegal is hard to surmise.

The effect of the Ferrari exclusion had been that McLaren became double World Champions overnight – even if the Woking team failed to score in Suzuka and Ferrari scored maximum points, they had enough to take the constructors' title as well.

Former barrister Mosley, who had been the letter 'M' of March cars, possessed more experience of race car building than any other previous FIA president. He took a good look at the barge board once back in his Paris office. 'It was immediately obvious that if the board had been at a slight angle to the

ABOVE: Eddie Irvine leads Mika Häkkinen in the controversial 1999 Malaysian Grand Prix in Sepang. Post-race, McLaren were awarded both championships until the FIA intervened ...

chassis [which it wasn't], rather than vertical, the dimension would have been legal because the shadow would have been smaller.' Charlie Whiting, who could have verified if the barge board had been vertical when it was attached to the car was conveniently on holiday. 'Someone from Ferrari came to check the boards prior to the appeal hearing and sure enough, they noticed the same thing,' Max wrote.

Ferrari won the appeal and now led both championships going into the final race. As a bizarre footnote, one of the cleaners at FIA headquarters then took it upon themselves to clean the race debris off the barge board, converting a piece of historic F1 memorabilia into a nondescript bit of carbon fibre.

McLaren weighed up all the scenarios of Mika versus Eddie versus Michael. Schumacher had taken pole, Mika alongside him, with Irvine back in fifth place

'The great strength of Mika was, first of all, his self-confidence and self-belief, and he just didn't seem to be affected by pressure,' Adrian told Tom Clarkson. 'I do remember in Suzuka, you had these little offices above the pits and on Saturday evening before the race, Ron Dennis, myself, Mika, the other key race engineers sat in that office upstairs, coming up with strategy. It became very complicated: "If Irvine pits here, then we do that, if Schumacher does that, we do this, and blah blah blah." Mika was just sitting quietly in the corner saying nothing. He just got up and left and the following morning he got in the car, disappeared into the distance, and won the race. That was Mika's way of doing things. He kept things simple.'

It wasn't quite Groundhog Day, though. Mika had won the drivers' title, but thanks to Ferrari's Malaysian re-instatement for an illegal car, McLaren had lost the constructors' championship. That didn't stop them partying like it was 1999.

Falling short

With Max Mosley satisfied that his new regulations were keeping car development in check, the rules changed very little in the first season of the new millennium. Thus Adrian Newey was able to produce the MP4/15 as an evolution of the previous year's car. Yet again it turned into a season of McLaren vs Ferrari, Häkkinen vs Schumacher, although this year the German would be aided by new team-mate Rubens Barrichello. Eddie Irvine had landed himself a big-money contract with Jaguar for 2000.

At this point in their history, Jaguar road cars was owned by Ford. It was Jackie Stewart's son Paul who had run a successful F3000 team in the 1990s, which had joined the F1 grid as Stewart Grand Prix in 1996, running Ford Cosworth engines. Jackie enjoyed a long association with Ford, so it seemed a logical step for Ford to buy the team (they already owned Cosworth) and promote their luxury car brand. The man they put in charge, Neil Ressler, had limited experience of Formula

LEFT: The launch of the McLaren MP4/15 in 2000. Reserve driver Olivier Panis stands in between DC and Mika.

RIGHT: Mika Häkkinen takes stock on the podium at Spa having been centimetres away from an 190mph accident of Michael Schumacher's making.

LEFT: Mika Häkkinen takes the Rettifilo chicane at Monza in 2000, the days when it was a left-right (today it is a right-left).

BELOW: Bobby Rahal (left) and Neil Ressler on the Suzuka pitwall at the Japanese Grand Prix in 2000. Ford had dropped them into the 'piranha tank' of ruthless team bosses.

BELOW RIGHT: One of the chief piranhas, Ron Dennis, was about to adopt a tough negotiating stance with his chief designer.

1. He'd acted as non-executive director of Stewart Grand Prix but little else. In January 2000 he was named chairman of Jaguar Racing, and he ran the team alongside fellow Ohioan, Bobby Rahal, who was equally inexperienced in the ways of 'the Piranha Club'.

McLaren appeared to have lost their edge after two years of success, while Ferrari were increasingly spurred on by a frustrated Italian media who wondered when the Todt/Brawn/Schumacher team were going to claim a title, having started their journey in 1996. The MP4/15 delivered a 1–2 in Britain and Spain, but five victories for Michael in the first eight races had given him a championship buffer of more than two race wins as they headed to Magny Cours in France.

Three Schumacher retirements later and the title race was back on. As the cars lined up at

Spa for the Belgian Grand Prix, Mika led Michael by two points. The race produced the overtaking move of the season, perhaps the decade.

In a wet/dry race Häkkinen was closing down leader Schumacher on Lap 40 of a 44-lap race. Towing up behind the Ferrari on the long Kemmel straight the McLaren moved to the inside line, at which point Schumacher made a late move to block, pushing Mika momentarily onto the grass and damaging his front wing with his rear tyre. It was a reckless manoeuvre that could have seen the McLaren spinning into the scenery at 190mph. The following lap Häkkinen again got close through Eau Rouge, but this time round they were approaching backmarker Ricardo Zonta's BAR-Honda. As Zonta moved to the centre of the track to let the leaders through Schumacher went one side and Häkkinen, making full use of the tow, went the other and was through to the lead. It was a move of immense bravery. After the race Mika visited Michael in the garage and told him in understated but determined tones that he would *never* be trying his Lap 40 blocking move again.

From there the McLaren season fizzled out. Schumacher won the next race in Italy and the three remaining races. Ferrari celebrated their first drivers' title since 1979 with no intervention needed from the blazers in Place de la Concorde. It would be the start of the dominant 'Dream team' era, when all the Scuderia resources and strategy choices were made to benefit the No.1 contracted driver and the full resources of Ferrari were lavished on the cars.

Jaguar and 2000

Having delivered a chassis which brought them renewed success in 1998 and 1999 with a near-miss in 2000, Newey was expecting a generous uplift at the next round of contract talks. He was cruelly mistaken. Ron Dennis was a negotiator who had many years' experience battling salary demands from Ayrton Senna, a similarly single-minded resolute individual. One year Ayrton held out until the start of the season and would

only drive on a race-by-race basis. Newey was shocked when he was offered a pay cut for the next contract cycle.

While this was happening, Bobby Rahal got in touch. Now installed as Jaguar team boss, he was looking for personnel to take the team forward. Many elements of what Newey looks for in a new team were present – a good personal relationship with the boss, in this case a man he had race-engineered for two years. He needed the team to be financially stable, Jaguar were backed by Ford, and he wanted to join a team where he could make a real difference, Jaguar had finished 9th out of 11 teams in 2000. The salary being offered was far in excess of what Ron Dennis was prepared to give him to keep him on board. Things got so advanced that Marigold was involved in negotiating terms and an outline letter of agreement was signed for Newey to start in August 2002.

The following morning, Adrian dropped into the office to tell Ron he was leaving to join Jaguar. He promptly took the afternoon off and took his two older daughters to the cinema, turning his phone off. While he was immersed in darkness, Dennis did some rapid recalculation of his salary scales. That evening

OPPOSITE: Alexander Wurz (centre) joined the driver line-up for the 2001 launch. Mercedes engine boss, Norbert Haug, is on the right.

ABOVE: David Coulthard is congratulated by Mika Häkkinen after picking up a podium in the 2001 Hungarian GP, as well as a sufficient amount of marbles on his tyres.

Ron and his personable wife Lisa descended on the Neweys in a charm offensive.

Dennis was quick to point out that with Niki Lauda now involved in the senior management structure of Jaguar, it might not be long before Newey was answering to the Austrian instead of Rahal. He also held out the olive branch that Newey might be allowed to take on side projects, such as an America's Cup yacht design. Plus, of course, his salary was boosted considerably.

The argument was won and Adrian accepted, though there was considerable fallout in the Newey–Rahal relationship and Ford were incensed. There was also a legal battle based on the letter of intent he had signed. Dennis chose to tackle it head on and addressed the media at the 2001 Canadian Grand Prix.

'I would much rather sit here now talking about how we tried to keep one of our best guys,' he told reporters. 'It is better than talking about why Adrian left us. Adrian has called me and he said, "I am happy to stay and you guys convinced me." So, we did a good job in the end.'

Asked if the incident had changed their relationship Ron admitted that it had. 'Life changes on a daily basis, so, yes, it has changed. Not for the better or for the worse. It has just changed. I don't think there has been any appreciable difference in our business relationship or our friendship.'

Life had changed. Newey's second contract period would be different from the first. Dennis made sure his bluff could not be called again by tasking Martin Whitmarsh to devise a new management system. No single employee could wield so much influence again. Whitmarsh put in place a 'matrix' structure, by any other name 'management-by-committee'. It was not going to suit a radical, out-of-the-box thinker like Adrian. He described it as an 'unnecessarily complex and wretchedly unworkable system of department heads and "performance creators" informally known as the mullahs after the Muslim scholars.'

However, Ron was right about one thing. Soon after the dust from Adriangate settled, Rahal was ousted from the Jaguar team and Niki Lauda took control.

Life in the 'Matrix'

The 2001 season with the MP4-16 yielded four wins and second place in the constructors' championship, but the bell curve of Ferrari success was still on the way up. Schumacher won his fourth World Championship with almost double the points total of second-place David Coulthard.

The MP4-17 of 2002 – the first produced by 'the matrix' engineering team – suffered badly from reduced engine power and reliability. Kimi Räikkönen, who had replaced the retiring Mika Häkkinen, suffered 10 DNFs in 17 races. This was the year that Ferrari were at their most dominant, with Michael Schumacher getting booed off the Austrian GP podium in early May when he had already won four of the first five races, yet the team obliged Rubens Barrichello to hand over that win as well. He was World Champion by July. At least the solitary McLaren win came in Monaco, where David Coulthard claimed the honours.

Given the scale of the competitive mountain they had to climb with the 2003 car, the MP4-18, Newey decided it was time for a radical new design with tightly

ABOVE: Räikkönen's McLaren MP4-17 leads Rubens Barrichello at the 2002 Monaco Grand Prix.

ABOVE RIGHT: The award-winning McLaren Technology Centre viewed in 2013 after the addition of the McLaren Production Centre (right).

RIGHT: Kimi Räikkönen arrived at McLaren in 2002

packaged aero. Although the brave new world of the Norman Foster-designed McLaren Technology Centre (MTC) 'the metropolis', may not have been to Adrian's liking, he did appreciate the state-of-the-art wind tunnel. Once in it he became concerned that the scale model he produced was giving great numbers in the wind tunnel while proving unstable on the test track. The lack of conclusive progress meant that in 2003 they raced an updated 2002 car, the MP4-17D.

It was a lot more competitive than the team had expected, especially in the hands of Räikkönen. Kimi scored six podiums in the first seven races, including a win in Malaysia – while DC took his one and only win in the opening race in Melbourne. Leaving Monaco, Kimi held a four-point lead over Michael Schumacher, so

WARSTEINER
SIEMENS

MILD SEVEN

LEFT: Giancarlo Fisichella (Jordan) receives the Brazilian GP winner's trophy from Kimi Räikkönen at Imola after the Finn was wrongly awarded victory at Interlagos in 2003, following an FIA miscalculation. Critics point out that the same procedure should have been adopted for Abu Dhabi 2021.

RIGHT: Future team-mates Mark Webber (Jaguar) and David Coulthard battle it out at the 2003 German Grand Prix at Hockenheim.

LEFT: The start of the 2003 European Grand Prix at the Nürburgring with Kimi Räikkönen leading the BMW-Williams of Ralf Schumacher.

there was no reason to rush the troublesome MP4-18 into action.

Into the drivers' fight stormed Juan Pablo Montoya in the Williams-BMW, with Fernando Alonso in the Renault not far behind. It was just what F1 needed. Following the dismal 2002 season of total Schumacher dominance TV ratings had plunged.

'At about the season's mid-point, the World Champions, Ferrari, started to go backwards,' wrote Richard Williams in the *Guardian*. 'In Hungary ten days ago, Fernando Alonso's Michelin-shod Renault [Ferrari ran Bridgestone] actually lapped Schumacher's Ferrari, an event so grave that for a minute it felt as though it might lead to the fall of the Italian government.'

Max Mosley had never been a fan of Michelin boss Edouard Michelin after he opposed him in the FIA presidential race, and he saw an opportunity to score points against the tyre supplier.

'Now it has been announced by the FIA that Michelin's tyres are apparently infringing the regulations in a curious manner,' Williams wrote. 'When a Michelin-shod car goes round a corner, its front tyres roll in such a way that a small part of their sidewalls come into contact with the track, increasing what the designers call the "contact patch" and improving the car's grip. It is claimed that this takes the width of the tyres beyond the permitted maximum of 270mm. As a result, the Michelin-contracted teams have been warned that they may be liable to future

LEFT: DC has an oversteery moment at Monza in 2004. Coulthard failed to score a podium in his final season with McLaren, while his team-mate took a solitary win at Silverstone.

RIGHT: Kimi Räikkönen in the McLaren MP4-19 turns in to Tabac at Monaco in 2004 pursued by Michael Schumacher (Ferrari).

disqualification – at, say, next week's Italian Grand Prix at Monza, where Ferrari are traditionally expected to produce results ...

'Michelin says it has supplied the same tyres at all the season's 13 races. So why, given Formula 1's notorious attention to technical minutiae, was this anomaly not spotted before?'

Why indeed. Mosley and Whiting had actually visited Maranello the week before the announcement, but in a characteristic patrician dismissal, Max said that tyres were only discussed 'in passing'.

Montoya exited the title race in the penultimate grand prix, but going to Suzuka – the finishing line for so many F1 championships - Räikkönen had an outside chance of the drivers' title. He needed to win and for Schumacher not to score a single point. That didn't look likely until Michael qualified down in 14th place. Pressure can easily distort a driver's natural ability; team-mate Barrichello was on pole. In the race, Schumacher was looking to stay out of trouble but in trying to overtake Takuma Sato, hit the Japanese driver's rear wheel and lost his front wing. This forced him to pit and he rejoined in last place. Schumacher narrowly avoided repeating the same accident at the chicane when brother Ralf ran into the back of him. He eventually finished in eighth place and scored a single championship point, with Kimi failing to get past Barrichello and coming home second. It had been a brave attempt with a revised 2002 car, but McLaren had slipped to third in the constructors' championship.

Arguments

The full limitations of the 'matrix' system became evident to Newey in 2004. Assisted by Peter Prodromou, and after many hours spent in the wind tunnel, Adrian now believed that the tricky MP4-18 needed a reshaped chassis and sidepod. The alternative view from the 'mullahs' of McLaren's engineering department was that it should be possible to revise the car, as they had done with the MP4-17. At a heated 'committee' meeting Martin Whitmarsh put it to the vote. Newey's idea was sidelined in favour of the revision route. Newey's anger was uncontained and he admitted he behaved very badly. But he knew they were making a mistake.

The car was launched as the MP4-19 and recorded eight DNFs out of the first 14 starts, McLaren's worst start to the season for many years. As the team

struggled on they dropped to fifth place in the constructors' table and by the time of the Belgian Grand prix at Spa they had amassed 37 points to runaway leaders Ferrari, who had 202.

Ron Dennis had finally agreed to a new chassis build with new aero and suspension, as per the Newey recommendations. The MP4- 19B was still missing Newey's intended cooling system, but its debut allowed Kimi Räikkönen to win at a track where he always excelled. In the hullabaloo that followed Michael Schumacher's seventh drivers' title, the news story that McLaren were back was slightly lost, but it gave Adrian enormous satisfaction.

Cars were getting too fast again and despite his indignation at having his ideas passed over by committee for the 2004 car, the 2005 design, the MP4-20,

LEFT: The driver line-up for 2005 and the vastly improved MP4-20. Norbert Haug anchors one end of the line next to reserve driver Pedro de la Rosa, Räikkönen and new signing Juan Pablo Montoya.

RIGHT: Kimi Räikkönen finished the 2005 season runner-up to Fernando Alonso and the team finished just nine points shy of Renault in the constructors' championship.

would be an interesting aero challenge. The FIA had restricted various elements, the crucial change being the 50mm lift in height of the front wing. Everything flowed from the front wing and so a change in height necessitated a change in the structures behind.

Adrian spent his summer holiday in Barbados mulling over front-wing tip vortices and front-lower wishbones. He became a regular visitor to the hotel's reception, clutching drawings to be faxed and scribbling on drawings that were faxed back. Marigold was not impressed.

But the result when it emerged, complete with a sidepod design that was unlikely to be copied over the course of a season, combined with a revolutionary double-clutch gearbox (from Tim Goss and Ivor Wood), was impressive. Räikkönen, now teamed with Juan Pablo Montoya, was quick in testing, though the Renault R25, in the hands of Fernando Alonso, was quickest.

It was a slow start to the year as the race engineers evolved the best set-up of the MP4-20. In a bid to force teams to save money, race engines were now required to last two races and the Mario Illien-produced Mercedes engines, as far as Newey was concerned, had far too many technical glitches. Nevertheless, as the season progressed, the car got more and more competitive. Räikkönen won in Spain, Monaco and Canada and was P2 on the grid for the ill-fated 2005 United States Grand Prix, when all the Michelin runners were forced to pull out due to multiple failures in practice.

Another regulation for 2005 had been that tyres must last the entire race distance, and Bridgestone had produced rubber that lasted a race distance but with poor performance, 'those Bridgestones were more like stones', recalled Ferrari press officer Luca Colajanni. Given that Michelins were failing on the high-speed Indy corners, there was a move to add a chicane and other compromise solutions, all of which were rejected by Ferrari boss Jean Todt. Max Mosley and the FIA would not intervene and the race weekend turned into an expensive fiasco, a 1–2 for Ferrari and a 5–6 for the delighted Minardi team, as only six cars competed.

In the second half of the season, the McLaren was the faster car, winning 10 of the 19 races. Räikkönen outscored Alonso in the last seven races of the season including a heroic win in Suzuka from 17th on the grid, but the drivers' title was already beyond him. Alonso made the overtaking move of the season in that same race, passing Michael Schumacher on the outside of the fearsome 130R (before it was modified).

The team lost the constructors' trophy to Renault by a mere nine points, but for Adrian the greater loss was his maverick independence to the matrix system of management. It was time to move on.

TOP LEFT: Martin Whitmarsh with Ron Dennis. The second time Newey told the McLaren boss he was leaving, there was no charm offensive.

ABOVE: Newey's parting shot, the MP4-21 in its testing livery. It would score no wins in 2006.

6

Red Bull
RENAULT
TOTAL
Red Bull

RED BULL 2005–2013

One of the most fascinating aspects of Formula 1 is the cloak-and-dagger attempts to hire top drivers and engineers while they are still working for other teams. Adrian's courtship by Christian Horner and Helmut Marko was more interesting than most.

Red Bull had been high-profile sponsors of the Sauber team since the mid-1990s, but were keen to take the next step into team ownership. The company was headed by marketing professional Dietrich Mateschitz, who had spotted the potential of the Red Bull drink on a trip to Thailand and grown the brand exponentially. When the floundering Jaguar team had come up for sale during the 2004 season as part of Ford's global restructuring, Red Bull bought them out.

The Austrian drinks firm magnate had been a boyhood fan of two great Austrian drivers, Jochen Rindt, F1's only posthumous World Champion, and his friend Helmut Marko, whose driving career was cut short by an injury at the 1972 French GP in Clermont Ferrand. Marko had already won Le Mans and set lap records at the Targa Florio in Sicily before a fateful stone was shot backwards through his helmet visor. Mateschitz tasked Marko with finding a suitable team boss for the new F1 outfit – Helmut had experience of running an F3000 team, RSM Marko. He had also once sold a racing trailer to Christian Horner, the boyish-looking, self-confident boss of the highly competitive Arden team (who won the F3000 championship in 2004). The two had stayed in touch and it was Christian who Marko recommended to take charge.

Adrian already had a trusted contact inside the Red Bull team. David Coulthard was ousted from McLaren in 2005 to make way for Juan Pablo Montoya and he added his considerable experience to the Red Bull driver line-up – the pairing of Vitantonio Liuzzi and Christian Klein were competent, but not

PREVIOUS PAGE: Mark Webber ploughs through the rain at the 2009 Chinese Grand Prix in Shanghai.

BELOW LEFT: Red Bull founder Dietrich Mateschitz pictured in 2006.

BELOW: David Coulthard at the wheel of the Newey's first RB chassis, the RB3 in 2007.

race winners, unlike DC, who scored a 4th place on his Red Bull debut.

Horner had already begun the 'small chats' with Adrian through the 2005 season, but then at Silverstone, as Newey was making his way through the paddock, he was approached by a tall Austrian in a leather jacket. 'I am Dr Helmut Marko. I work for Red Bull. You will give me a ring,' Adrian recalled. At which point he handed him his card. Since 2005, Helmut's direct approach to so many things has become legend in the paddock, but Newey was startled by this first meeting. It all made sense – the attention from Horner, the approach from Marko.

Fearing that any conspicuous contact with another team might have Ron Dennis's Ringwraiths descending upon him at speed, Adrian agreed to a secret visit to Red Bull HQ in Salzburg. Christian, DC and Marigold came along for the trip, where Mateschitz showed off his amazing aviation collection. It was all going along nicely until Marigold, who was negotiating on behalf of her

husband, indicated the salary he would require (estimated by *GP Racing* in 2007 as $10m). It was no more than he was earning at McLaren, but it had a chilling effect on Mateschitz and his advisor. Had they not checked what the pay grade would be for a multiple World Championship-winning designer?

A quick phone call to Gerhard Berger was all that was needed to convince his fellow Austrians that this was a golden opportunity. It was a deal. After the final race in China on 16 October, he let Ron know his decision. This time there were

no pleas for him to stay, though Dennis did want him to hold off the departure announcement. When Adrian refused to delay, he returned to his desk only to be told to gather his things (not that Ron Dennis allowed many 'things' in the MTC) and leave the building. It was a shocking farewell. Twenty years on, when Newey left the Red Bull organisation, they handled his departure immeasurably better.

Although Adrian relished the challenge of a new team, hungry for success with great financial backing, there were considerable hurdles to overcome when he arrived at the former Jaguar HQ in Milton Keynes on 1 March, 2006. There was no wind tunnel and no driver-in-the-loop simulator, what's more the team were being supplied with a reduced-spec Ferrari 056 engine. A meeting with Jean Todt failed to get them upgraded to the factory spec.

Inertia

A more fundamental problem was an attitude among some of the staff which – for a technocrat who shied away from man management duties – was potentially problematic. 'The day I joined, we went out for lunch with the key engineering team,' he told the *High Performance* podcast. 'One of them said to me, "Adrian, we're delighted to have you here, but please be aware that we at Jaguar have our way of doing things, and we expect you to fit in."'

Newey was surprised that after a year as Red Bull Racing the reference point was still Jaguar, who had scored two third-place podiums across five seasons in F1 and had come seventh in the 2004 constructors' championship.

'I don't actually have a problem with that. I'm happy to fit in, but the underlying implication was very strange. I'd been lucky enough to win quite a few championships at Williams and McLaren by then, and you'd think they would have been curious as to pick my brains and what I could bring in, what my experiences were. There was none of that. It took us a year to kind of change that culture.'

Once he'd started, he was aware that this resistance to the Newey direction of travel was slowing up the changes he wanted to make.

'I felt that there were four or five bad eggs in the team. And I just had the impression they were saying "yes" to my face and running around and saying "no" to my back and getting various people to push in the opposite direction. So I actually asked a very good family friend who worked in the hotel industry to come and work at Red Bull as a consultant, three days a week. She was a sort of undercover HR super-consultant, if you like.

'And after a month or two, she came back, and it was actually the same four

LEFT: A top view of the RB3 as it leaves the pit lane during testing at Jerez in February 2007.

or five people [he'd suspected]. Unfortunately we had to get rid of those people. But I tell you what, the culture changed overnight from that.'

To help move things along, Adrian was able to recruit Peter Prodromou, Ivor Wood and also Paul Monaghan who he had worked with in his early years at McLaren. Monaghan joined as Head of Race Engineering, although Adrian tasked him with a wider role of liaising with the FIA over rule changes – and delaying them as much as he could so that Red Bull could get their design and engineering up to speed.

Horner may have wanted Newey to nudge the 2006 car, the RB2, into a better window given that David Coulthard managed to score the team's first podium at the Monaco Grand Prix, but Adrian's sole focus was on 2007 and the RB3, as he told *GP Racing*. 'From my own point of view I spent some time trying to understand the RB2, the different philosophies that had gone into it. But I felt that to give the RB3 its best chance I needed to start to put into place what we all agreed were the system changes we needed to implement.'

It all starts with RB3

Newey found certain aspects of the RB2's development path wanting and went back to the clean sheet of paper. This was unusual in the third year of a stable set of aerodynamic regulations when most of the other cars on the grid had taken small steps rather than opt for radical change.

What was imperative, though, was to get a better spec engine than the one he knew to be downgraded. Rob White at Renault agreed to supply them with an engine with the same output as the works team. This enabled Red Bull to transfer the Ferrari engine supply to the newly minted Toro Rosso team.

The Minardi family name had a long association with motorsport; Giancarlo Minardi's grandfather had run a Fiat dealership in Faenza since 1927. After competing in a number of series, the team had been F1's plucky losers for twenty years, ultimately selling out to Aussie aviation entrepreneur Paul Stoddart who ran the company from Ledbury (Herefordshire) and Faenza. When sponsorship had dried up he had sold Minardi to Red Bull as their second team to promote drivers who had risen through its young driver programme, Red Bull Driver Search. In 2007 they would swap their customer Cosworth engines for Ferrari units – quite convenient considering Faenza's proximity to Maranello.

Apart from getting the factory organised, enlarging the engineering department and designing the new RB3, Adrian had the job of providing Toro

RED BULL RACING WINS AND PODIUMS MANHATTAN

Displayed in graphic form, the wins and podium placings for the Red Bull team show the dramatic fall-off in results at the introduction of the hybrid era in 2014.

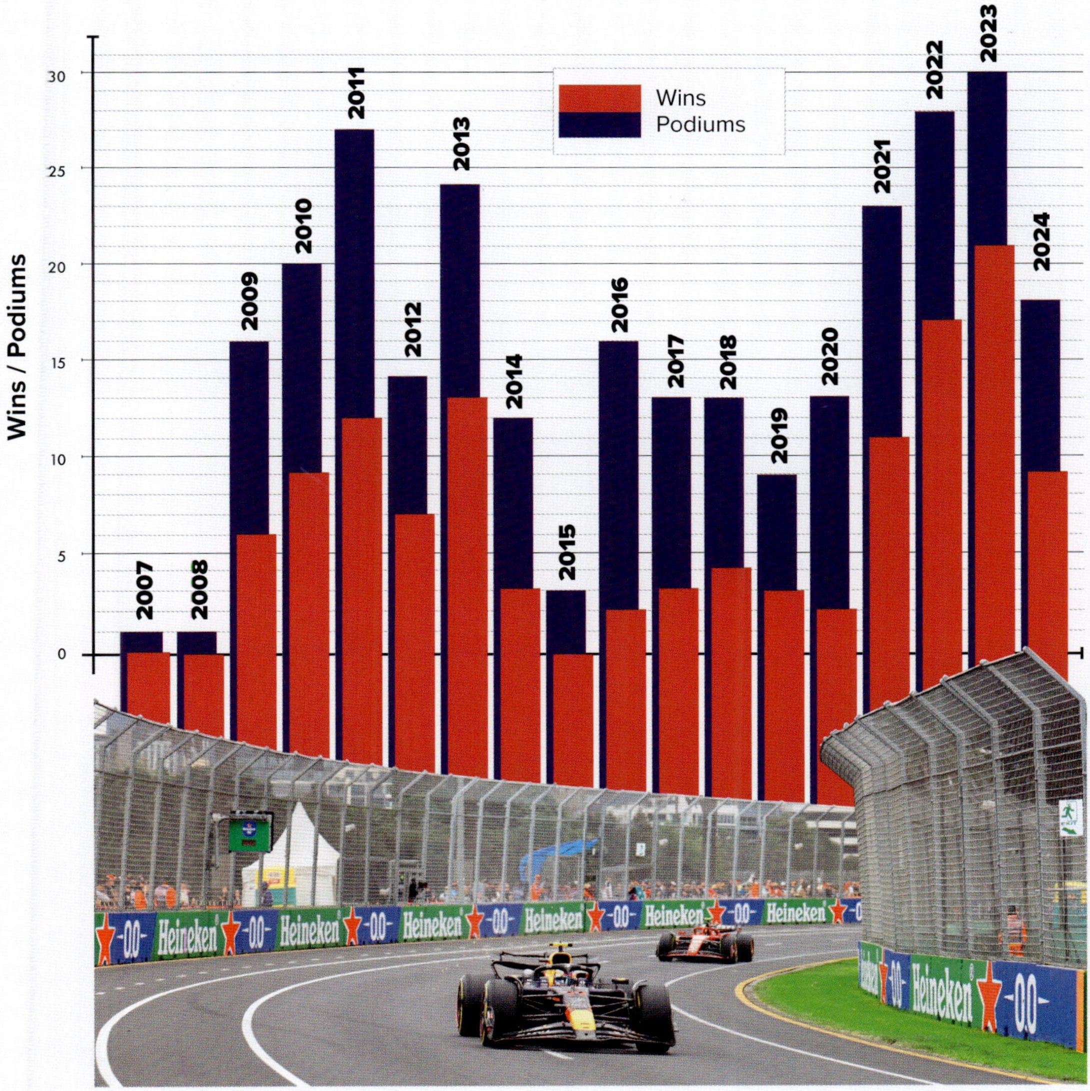

Red Bull
GIVES YOU WINGS
RAUCH
RAUCH
MAGNETI MARELLI

LEFT: A front-on comparison between the Red Bull RB3, with DC at the wheel, and the Toro Rosso STR2 of Sebastian Vettel (below), driving at the 2007 Turkish Grand Prix. Newey's RB design was doing double duty with the team from Faenza and rival teams were not happy.

Rosso with a new chassis as well. The cars would differ thanks to the mounting of their two different engines, but would ostensibly be the same.

In January 2007, *Autosport*'s Jonathan Noble revealed, 'Toro Rosso are set to run a development version of the Adrian Newey-designed RB3 chassis that Red Bull Racing will also compete with in 2007. Those plans have upset some rival teams, who have threatened legal action if the team go ahead with the scheme because they claim that outfits must design and build those cars.'

Gerhard Berger was the boss of Toro Rosso at the time. He pointed out that Newey was an employee of Red Bull Technologies not Red Bull Racing. Red Bull Technologies had not signed the Concorde Agreement which mandated teams to produce their own cars and therefore was free to supply more than one team with car designs and parts. 'We are confident the FIA will approve our car,' said Berger. 'The STR2 will be built by Red Bull Technologies, and Toro Rosso will fully own the intellectual rights of the car.'

It would likely have made Adrian uncomfortable exploiting that particular loophole, considering he had pointed out the Benetton and Ligier similarities in the past, but the (2007) STR2, the (2008) STR3 and (2009) STR4 are designs credited to him and his design team. Most interesting of all, it was his STR3 in the hands of Sebastian Vettel who scored the Red Bull organisation's first pole and first win. It's a fact that Gerhard Berger has enjoyed sharing with Christian Horner repeatedly.

At the Autosport International show in January 2007 (before the RB3 had run in testing) Adrian was keen to play down expectations. 'Red Bull is a young team and that was part of the attraction of joining them. You could say they're an old team, just Jaguar rebadged, but that really isn't the case. On the engineering side I'd say that over 50 per cent of the staff are post-Jaguar. The workforce are tremendously talented in all areas but we haven't really had long to get to know each other. And, equally, we don't yet have the resources of an established team.

'Red Bull have a healthy budget, but this myth that's being put about by some of the other team owners that we're big spenders – the Chelsea of F1 – is total tripe. I certainly wouldn't use budget as an excuse if we don't perform. We've grown rapidly already. Now we need a period of stability while we put all the systems in place.'

Staff at the Red Bull Racing team now numbered around 450, up from the 50 employees of March in the late 1980s, but less than the 550 at McLaren.

The first season with incoming Mark Webber partnering David Coulthard in the RB3, brought a solo podium at the European Grand Prix and fifth place in the

constructors' championship. Yet again reliability was an issue, with seven DNFs each for the drivers.

RB4 fails to deliver

The following year's RB4 could benefit from no big regulation changes. Red Bull scored a solitary podium and were overtaken by the previously dismal Toyota team, who had burned through a pile of money to ascend from tenth place in the 2002 constructors' championship to fifth place in 2008 (before exiting from the sport at the end of 2009 courtesy of the global financial crisis). What was worse, the Milton Keynes team had been beaten by the smaller outfit in Faenza.

Red Bull protégé Sebastian Vettel, driving for Toro Rosso, had made the most of the wet conditions and taken pole for the Italian Grand Prix at Monza. He had broken the record for the youngest polesitter, while Red Bull cars occupied three of the first four grid spots. Few expected Sebastian to hang on to the lead once the red lights went out, but in an equally wet race, the 21-year-old resisted all pressure to become the youngest grand prix winner of all time. It was a stratospheric result and Adrian's third winning marque. However, the downside

LEFT: David Coulthard guns his RB4 through Parabolica at Monza in September 2008.

ABOVE: Sebastian Vettel threads his 'RB4 equivalent', the Toro Rosso STR3, through the Rettifilo chicane on his way to a surprise victory.

ABOVE RIGHT: The Toro Rosso team, with many old hands from Minardi days, celebrate their first ever win ... and the first for the Red Bull organisation.

was that Dietrich Mateschitz demanded that Red Bull Milton Keynes get their act together. Comparisons with Toyota were onerous.

Part of the reason that the RB4 was under-developed was the impending rules change for 2009. Whereas the front wing would be the full width of the car, the rear wing would now be taller and narrower, giving the cars a distinctly ugly look viewed head-on. The changes had been made with the aim to generate more overtaking, as F1 was suffering from the perennial problem of cars being unable to follow closely because of too much dirty air. Gone were the days when Max Mosley espoused the view that F1 races should be like chess matches and that overtaking on track was irrelevant.

With Adrian at the height of his powers during a regulations change, most of his attention was devoted to the RB5 of 2009 and Mateschitz would have to be reassured that change was soon to come.

2009: Progress at last!

Given his meteoric performances of 2008, one of the key changes for 2009 came in the Red Bull driver line-up with Helmut Marko keen to see his staircase of talent prove successful.

Sebastian Vettel would push Mark Webber a lot harder than DC and, though Adrian had enormous respect for David Coulthard, who had become more of a friend than a colleague, Vettel exhibited many of the inquisitive aspects of Ayrton Senna. He was the one driver to visit the Pirelli factory once they took over as sole tyre supplier in 2011.

When the cars were unveiled Newey was hoping that his innovative approach to the RB5's diffuser combined with a pullrod suspension would pay dividends. What he wasn't expecting was for three teams – Williams, Brawn and Toyota – to interpret the rules more radically. An engineer at Honda (which transitioned to become Brawn) had spotted a loophole that enabled the car to effectively have a double diffuser, greatly increasing rear downforce.

ABOVE: A chilly launch for the RB5 at Jerez in 2009. With Adrian's systems now in place, the team were about to make progress.

F1 designers work at the boundaries of permissibility and Adrian was convinced this was illegal, as someone who'd missed a key performance loophole might. It was a view shared by the top teams. On the Wednesday before the season-opening race in Australia, an official complaint was launched by the seven non-diffuser teams citing the Williams FW31, Brawn BGP 001 and Toyota TF109. The FIA scrutineers disagreed and threw the challenge out.

The Brawn team had only got to the grid thanks to the generosity of Honda and a lifeline handed to the team by McLaren's Martin Whitmarsh. Exiting the sport at speed in the global recession, Honda withdrew from F1 in 2008 leaving drivers Jenson Button and Rubens Barrichello without a drive for 2009 and the grid reduced to 18 cars. Ross

Brawn had persuaded Honda to finance the team for the start of the season and Whitmarsh had supplied them with a Mercedes engine – little knowing that McLaren were about to be outcompeted by a team that was half in the lifeboat.

It was one of Formula 1's great comeback stories that unfolded over the course of the year, with the Honda/Brawn interpretation of the double diffuser rules paying huge dividends in the early races of the season and Jenson Button taking the lead in the drivers' championship. Button won six of the first seven races, the exception being China when the RB5 came good in the wet, Sebastian Vettel's favourite track condition. Mark Webber shared the podium in third place and Christian Horner joined them for the silverware.

'It was a massive thing to go and pick up the constructors' trophy [in China], even though it was broken and missing one of its handles!' Horner recalled. 'It was a huge moment to look down and see the emotion of the team, to see Helmut almost crying, to see the faces of every member of the team. I just remember the feeling of getting on the aeroplane still smelling of champagne, thinking that this moment has been so special and that we'd definitely need to feel that sensation more times in our careers.

'It was a big thing for us, because of the whole debate going on about double diffusers. Adrian, for example, wasn't at that race in China because he was back in the UK drawing our double diffuser that would make its debut at the Monaco Grand Prix.'

Red Bull had joined the footrace of F1 teams hastily adapting their cars to

BELOW LEFT: Sebastian Vettel leads Felipe Massa (Ferrari) at the 2009 Monaco GP.

BELOW: Helmut Marko's wunderkind scored the first Red Bull win in China despite the absence of the must-have item for 2009, a double diffuser.

BELOW RIGHT: Vettel won again at Silverstone, with Mark Webber taking victory in the following race at the Nürburgring.

Red Bull
TOTAL
RENAULT

Pepe Jeans

LEFT: Newey always favours evolution over revolution and the RB6 continued the strong form shown by the RB5, which won the second half of the 2009 season.

BELOW LEFT: Mark Webber rides the kerbs at the exit of the Swimming Pool chicane at Monaco on his way to victory in 2010.

BELOW: After the obligatory Red Bull pool dip, Mark and Seb both jumped into Monaco harbour – as Adrian wryly noted in his autobiography, that was the last time they would be holding hands ...

include a double diffuser, but the Monaco installation was rushed and Button won again. By the time of the British Grand Prix in July, Newey was satisfied that the gearbox and rear suspension had been properly repackaged. Vettel and Webber promptly delivered a crushing 1–2, over 40 seconds clear of Rubens Barrichello's Brawn. Adrian got up on the podium to pick up the constructors' trophy and celebrate a win for his fourth marque.

From Silverstone it was game on ... almost. Mark Webber won the next race in Germany, leading home another Red Bull 1–2, but results after that were patchy. That is until the final three races of the year, concluded in style with wins in Japan, Brazil and Abu Dhabi (the new final race of the season at the day/night Yas Marina circuit). The odds looked good for a strong challenge in 2010. The team finished second in the constructors' championship, with 153.5 points to Brawn's 172; their closest rivals in third place, McLaren, scored just 71. The 'party team' now had to be taken very seriously.

2010 – The Title Race

The 2010 season turned out to be a battle between Red Bull and Ferrari. Fernando Alonso had lost faith in his Renault team and moved to the Italian team – in part believing them to have the special 'luck' guaranteed them by being good friends with the FIA.

The largest regulation change was the ban on refuelling. It was done on safety and financial grounds in the wake of Toyota, Honda and BMW exiting the sport at speed and the very real danger (or opportunity) that the bigger teams might be obliged to run three cars to make up the grid, should smaller teams leave.

'I enjoy regulation changes. Stability makes F1 very stale,' Adrian told *Guardian* motorsport journalist Maurice Hamilton at the start of the year. 'The changes allow me to sit back with a fresh sheet of paper and work out solutions from first principles.

'The initial problem from the car design point of view for 2010 is a straightforward packaging problem. We've gone from having a fuel tank that holds about 90 kilos [117 litres] of fuel to needing one that holds about 160 kilos [210 litres], so almost double the size. And that means the car has got to be longer, and probably wider as well to minimise the extra length. But going wider means you reduce the radiator area. So it was a question of balancing the need for cooling with the fuel tank/car length.

'More difficult was how that affects the car dynamics in terms of ride height change from qualifying with little or no fuel, to the start of the race with 160 kilos on board. That brings a big ride height change, and that is critical to the car's performance. Then there are other factors, such as the extra tyre degradation brought about by the extra weight through the early part of the race and the fact that we have narrower front tyres, which means the cars tend to understeer.'

Heading into 2010 his ultra-competitive nature came to the fore, but it was clear from the swipe he took at Mercedes, and his old nemesis Ross Brawn, that he expected the challenge to come from Mercedes (who had bought out Brawn but kept him as team boss) and McLaren.

'The fact is the Mercedes engine enjoyed a good advantage over the rest of the field last year. Lap time-wise it was significant; several tenths of a second. When you have to try and claw that back in the chassis, it's quite a big ask. Mercedes developed very heavily through what was meant to be a frozen engine, whereas some of the others, Renault in particular, were very honest and said: "It's a frozen engine, it's cost cutting, we won't develop further." And they fell behind. But they have had a good programme to address that. As for what

BELOW LEFT: Christian Horner is pursued by the press pack after his drivers' collision in Turkey.

BELOW: Sebastian Vettel and Fernando Alonso in the Ferrari go side by side into the first turn at the Hungaroring in 2010.

Mercedes did last year, that's part of motorsport and you have to be philosophical about these things.'

In the end it proved to be a Ferrari F10 in the hands of Fernando Alonso, that would be Red Bull's main challenger in 2010. This was the year that Red Bull scored their first ever 1–2 at Monaco and the harbourside motorhome, the Energy Station, which contained a rooftop swimming pool, became the scene of what would become a traditional RBR post-win swimming 'gala'. Despite missing the first day of testing with the RB6 the team had already put in some strong performances, Vettel claiming his first win of 2010 at the third race, the Malaysian Grand Prix.

It was Mark Webber who had won in Monaco, following a win in Spain. At the top of the drivers' table it was now Mark and Sebastian equal on 78 points, with Alonso on 75 points as they headed for Istanbul Park.

Before the season, Adrian had enthused about the driver pairing: 'I think it's great! They're out to beat each other and that's the first thing you want in a pair of team-mates. If you have one driver that is significantly slower than the other, then the quicker driver starts to get complacent. We've seen that many times. Ayrton allowed himself to slip into that when Michael Andretti was his team-mate in 1993. It wasn't until Mika stepped into the second seat [towards the end of the season] that Ayrton upped his game.

'They push each other. I think the relationship between Seb and Mark is as good as two rivals will ever be. They help each other in terms of being open and honest during debriefs. We're looking to win the championship and we've got an excellent pair of drivers. I'm very happy with them.'

At the Turkish Grand Prix that all fell apart. Mark was leading from a fast-charging Sebastian as Vettel got the tow coming up the hill towards the braking zone of the final chicane. But as Seb's RB6 drew alongside, he suddenly edged across into Mark and the cars collided.

'As uncomfortable as it is to say it, I think there's no reason for Sebastian to be pulling right there,' said DC now installed in the TV commentary box. 'I'm giving it 100 per cent Vettel's fault,' added Martin Brundle. The cameras switched to the pit wall and Adrian Newey burying his head in his hands. 'I've never seen such an extreme reaction from Adrian Newey, he's appalled,' noted commentator Jonathan Legard.

Vettel's mistake had cost the team a 1–2 finish. Worse, Helmut Marko was of the opinion that Webber should not have crowded Vettel to the edge of the track, the accident was down to the Australian. For Mark it now became very clear that his team-mate was the favoured son.

'We ended up back in my office,' recalled Christian Horner. 'It was an

BELOW: Sebastian Vettel wins the final race of the season at Yas Marina to lead the championship for the first time all year.

RIGHT: Vettel leads Nico Rosberg at the 2011 Italian Grand Prix at Monza.

opportunity for Mark to get everything out, address his issues with Helmut. I said to Helmut before the meeting, "Whatever Mark says, take it on the chin and agree." And so Mark went through all the issues that had pissed him off about Helmut, blah, blah blah. Helmut took it all on board and said, "Yes, okay, I agree". And then he said, "Anyway, the next race in Valencia is very important to us and you've always been shit in Valencia!" Mark, thankfully, saw the funny side but it explains some of the straight talking that Helmut tends to have.'

Sadly, Helmut's prophecy about Valencia proved correct, but for unexpected reasons. The Red Bulls locked out the front row of the grid, and in the race Webber made an early pit stop for the medium compound tyres. Unusually, his pit crew botched the stop and he was stationary for 7.9 seconds, rejoining in 18th position. Now running behind the much slower Lotus of Heikki Kovalainen, he failed to estimate how much earlier the backmarker was braking and the RB6 slammed into his rear tyre, launching it airborne. It was a testament to the solidity of Newey's design that Webber was able to walk away from such a spectacular accident unhurt.

The season raged on with the German Grand Prix victory being gifted to Alonso after Felipe Massa's race engineer radioed in to his driver, 'Felipe, Fernando is faster than you'. The coded message to Massa to move over fooled no one and in the era of 'no team orders', Ferrari were fined $100,000 but kept the points.

At the penultimate race of the season in Brazil Red Bull had the opportunity to pull the same 'adjustment' to boost Webber's chances of catching Alonso in the title race, but Horner argued that as Seb still had a mathematical chance of winning the championship the cars should finish in their natural order of Vettel first and Webber second. It was enough to give them the constructors' title one race before the end of the season. There was celebration, but it was brief.

Coming into the final grand prix in Abu Dhabi there were four drivers in with a mathematical chance of winning the drivers' title, though Lewis Hamilton would have needed a demolition derby of his rivals to win. The bookies had Alonso as the overwhelming favourite. After Germany, the Spaniard's run of results had been 2nd, DNF, 1st, 1st, 3rd, 1st, 3rd. He had 246 points to Webber's 238 and Vettel's 231.

Vettel took a convincing pole position on Saturday evening with Alonso third fastest, and Webber only fifth. Finish in that order and Alonso would be an easy champ. But Fernando got a poor start, lost a place and found himself being trailed by Webber with Massa (who'd bungled his qualifying, lifting off on his final flyer when he momentarily thought he was out of time) behind. A pressure-free Vettel maintained the lead.

On Lap 8, while being chased by Massa, Webber brushed the barrier at the penultimate corner. 'Losing the rear tyres, mate, losing the rears,' he told Red Bull. Four laps later, with the Aussie struggling to find performance in his tyres, the team brought him in for a new set. He emerged seven seconds behind Russian driver Vitaly Petrov's Renault.

There was a peculiar characteristic of the Bridgestone tyre that the soft would degrade and lose pace then suddenly enter a 'cleaning phase'. If they were managed correctly, after a short lull, the pace would return. Ferrari brought Alonso in as all the front-runners were beginning to struggle. They wanted to cover off the undercut from Webber. Fernando came out behind the already-stopped Petrov, just in front of Mark ... and then couldn't get past.

Almost immediately, the front-runners who were going long found that their pace was picking up again and stayed out. Alonso was marooned in seventh place, needing to be fourth, and Webber was stuck behind Alonso. Vettel took the win but Christian Horner waited until Alonso had crossed the line before letting him know, 'Sebastian Vettel, you are World Champion!'

The upstart team were double World Champions. In the wild celebrations that followed Adrian Newey barely had time to register that he was now the only F1 designer to have won constructors' championships with three different F1 teams.

LEFT: Sebastian Vettel acknowledges the crowd at the Buddh International Circuit. Seb would dominate the three F1 races held in India.

BELOW: Adrian, Red Bull press officer Kate Tweedle and Christian Horner celebrate at Suzuka in 2011.

2011-2013: Easy, Hard, Easy

The major work on the RB7 centred around recovering the downforce lost when the FIA decided that double diffusers would no longer be allowed. The other significant change for 2011 was the re-introduction of the kinetic energy recovery system, KERS. This required the optimal placement of a heavy battery in the chassis. It gave an extra boost to help overtaking, but had a tendency to overheat – often the Achilles heel of tightly packaged Newey designs.

Adrian chose to split the battery into four units and place them between the engine and the gearbox, a wholly innovative approach but one that would be hard to replicate – his chief designer, Rob Marshall, who would go on to pen the 2024 McLaren, thought it impossible. Never a good word to bounce back at Newey. He got it to work.

'During the early part of the season the KERS system was in the habit of packing up and was constantly in danger of catching fire,' he wrote in his autobiography, 'but once we made it reliable, we had this underlying, baked-in advantage that we were able to carry for the balance of that season, a key part of the 2011, 2012 and 2013 championship-winning cars. Which, as you can imagine, appealed to my sense of continuity.'

TOTAL
RENAULT
GEOX
RedBull
RAUCH
TOTAL

PETRONAS

GEOX

LEFT: Mark Webber on the way to his second Monaco GP win in 2012, with the RB8, and Newey stepped up to the royal box to collect the race constructors' trophy.

BELOW LEFT AND RIGHT: Adrian evolved his podium technique over two seasons between 2011 and 2012. Given that Sebastian Vettel took great delight in spraying champagne into his eyes (2011) in 2012 he brought goggles.

To gain some of the precious downforce back, Newey routed the RB7's exhaust so it would blow hard on the now single diffuser. Exhaust blowing had been on his radar since 1994 and the Williams FW16. This time round he asked Renault to devise a system where the engine would be constantly blowing on the diffuser, even though the driver had lifted off for a corner. It maintained the downforce levels at the critical point of corner entry, cutting the actual power to the wheels through sophisticated engine mapping, but still maintaining what would be known as 'hot blowing'.

It was a season when the new 23-year-old World Champion Vettel stamped his authority in what proved to be a dominant car – Vettel won six of the opening eight races and five out of the final eight to become champion for a second time with a Schumacher-esque four races left on the calendar. He was 122 points ahead of second-place Jenson Button. The constructors' title was secured by a similar margin.

Ferrari, who had come close to the title in 2010, failed to show up for the fight in 2011. As Adrian drily noted, they couldn't get their own exhaust system to provide extra downforce, so tried to get the Red Bull and its slavishly copied counterpart on the McLaren banned. It was temporarily banned at Silverstone, but reinstated for the rest of the season.

The regulations for 2012 reflected the FIA's determination to get rid of 'off-throttle blown diffusers' and required cars to have exhausts exiting the bodywork in a far higher position than before. With the lowering of the nose heights, almost the entire grid adopted a stepped ('platypus') nose, making them look, in the words of Pirelli's Paul Hembery, 'pig ugly'. Hembery doubted that sponsors would want to attach their name to that end of the car. Outspoken former German F1 racer Hans-Joachim Stuck went further: 'The tyres are too narrow, the rear wing too small and the front wing too big, and the nose is a complete failure,' he said.

There was also a crackdown on exotic engine maps, though it didn't stop some teams trying to use the exhaust to create downforce. At the German Grand Prix in July, Red Bull Racing were referred to the race stewards after FIA Technical Delegate Jo Bauer noted that their engine maps had the potential to circumvent the technical regulations. They were suspected of manipulating the relationship between the torque produced by the RB8 and the degree to which the throttle was open – particularly in medium-speed corners. This allowed more air to pass through the exhaust and over the diffuser, generating downforce.

It was technically within the rules – as written – and the stewards took no

action but the governing body then tightened the regulations even further. They required teams to submit an engine map used during one of the first four races of the season, which became known as the 'reference map' to which their future race maps would be compared. As F1 journalist Andrew Davies noted, 'the FIA were playing "Whack-a-Mole" with F1's software engineers'.

In spite of the cars' awkward looks, pundits hailed the start of the 2012 season as a new dawn for the excitement and unpredictability of Formula 1. For once there was no runaway leader – remarkably there were seven different race winners in the first seven races, including Pastor Maldonado for Williams, who held off Fernando Alonso at his home race in Spain.

As teams exited the Italian Grand Prix in September, Alonso led the standings with 179 points, Vettel was only fourth with 140 points and Webber back on 132. Sebastian then rattled off four grand prix wins in a row, Singapore, Japan, South Korea and India. Over the three years that the race was run at the Buddh circuit, Vettel won in an Adrian Newey-designed car every time. That put Sebastian on 240 with Alonso now on 227, while Red Bull had a commanding lead in the constructors' championship.

Heading into the final race of the 20-race season in Brazil, Vettel led by 13 points and needed to finish fourth or better if Alonso won. Vettel only managed to qualify on the second row, but with Alonso back in eighth it looked as if careful race management would allow him to cruise to his third World Championship.

Mark Webber is great friends with Fernando Alonso ever since they were team-mates together with Jenson Button at Benetton in 2001. When the red lights

ABOVE LEFT: Seb on his recovery drive back to the points in the rain at Interlagos in 2012.

ABOVE: The start of the championship-deciding 2012 race in Brazil. Mark Webber moves to the inside where his team-mate is aiming to put his car, while Fernando Alonso sails around the outside.

RIGHT: A close up of the intricate detail on the front wing of the RB8 under the lights of Singapore in 2012.

went out, Webber was giving his 2012 team-mate no quarter and moved to the inside, squeezing Vettel against the pit wall. No team orders apparent! Sebastian had to back off into the melee that is Turn 1 at Interlagos and exited the corner in seventh place, with Alonso now ahead and up into fifth. Down the hill the cars plunged towards the high-speed Turn 4, Lake Descent. Sebastian took a wide line into the corner and tagged the Williams of Bruno Senna on the inside – he was spun round and hit, a large hole being punched into the RB8's sidepod. The car ended up rolling backwards down the hill, plumb last.

In rainy conditions with the track proving exceptionally slippery but not requiring full wets, Vettel began a rapid rise through the field. His ability in mixed conditions was unquestioned, the bigger question was could his battered car last until the end of the race? Frantic analysis of the damage was begun at mission control in Milton Keynes; photos of the sidepod and a squashed exhaust pipe were shared with the pit wall. The car looked safe to continue, but would it overheat, or even catch fire? Nico Hulkenberg made a rash overtaking move on race leader Lewis Hamilton on Lap 54 and suddenly Jenson Button was leading

with Alonso in P2, but Vettel had climbed his way to sixth place and heavy rain started to fall. After an accident with Paul di Resta's Force India brought out the safety car, the last three laps were run line astern and the World Championship sealed. Nerves had been shredded back at base, in the garage and on the pit wall. Red Bull had made it three in a row – drivers' and constructors' titles. The upstart team were on their way to emulating the Ferrari dominance under Todt and Brawn ... without imposing team orders.

ABOVE: Adrian Newey (armed with the famous notebook) and Christian Horner tackle Pirelli's Paul Hembery before the 2013 Hungarian Grand Prix.

TOP RIGHT: Sebastian Vettel in wet practice for the 2013 Brazilian Grand Prix.

RIGHT: The 2013 Malaysian Grand Prix marked another low point in the Vettel/Webber relationship. Seb ignored the discreet team order, 'multi 21', to hold station and attacked his team-mate ... as Mark reminded him in the press conference afterwards.

2013

If 2012 had been touch and go, then 2013 would turn out to be a demonstration run. Some of the cars had softened the Frankenstein nature of the platypus nose, but Newey was in no hurry to alter a championship-winning approach and the RB9 kept its stepped profile. This was the year where Pirelli came under strong criticism after a series of punctures at Silverstone.

A total of six tyre failures occurred during the British Grand Prix, including race leader Lewis Hamilton driving in his first season for Mercedes. Pirelli were forced to modify the compounds for the following German Grand Prix as a stop-gap solution before introducing a more robust tyre at the Hungarian Grand Prix. This reversion to a 2011-spec tyre fully suited the RB9, which in the hands of three-time World Champion Vettel was unbeatable. Sebastian strung together a record-breaking nine successive race victories to overload the trophy cabinet back at Milton Keynes and make it four straight doubles. But a major regulation change was coming in 2014, and for once Newey was not looking forward to it. The 'hybrid' era would place maximum emphasis on engine power not aero efficiency – the bad news was that championships would be won on the dyno, not in the wind tunnel.

ROKT
Red Bull
ORACLE
BYBIT
RAUCH

7

RED BULL 2014–2024

For those who thought Adrian Newey was embedded in Red Bull for life, the start of the 2014 season brought a shock to the system. This was the first year of the new hybrid engine formula, with turbocharged engines returning to the sport for the first time since 1988. The new engines were a 1.6-litre, V6 with an 8-speed semi-automatic gearbox. In this brave new world of energy recovery KERS played a far bigger role, renamed as ERS-K. Engines were now 'power units', consisting of an internal combustion engine (ICE); a Motor

BELOW: Despite an agonising lack of Renault power, Daniel Ricciardo managed to win the 2014 Belgian Grand Prix.

PREVIOUS PAGE: Max Verstappen rounds the Anthony Noghès corner at Monaco in 2023, the year Red Bull shredded the record books.

BELOW: Whereas the first phase of Red Bull belonged to Webber and Vettel, the second phase was enlivened by the partnership of Ricciardo and Verstappen.

Generator Unit-Kinetic (MGU-K), which harvested energy that would normally be lost under braking; Motor Generator Unit-Heat (MGU-H), which collected energy in the form of exhaust heat, all gathered together in the Energy Store (ES).

It was clear from the start that Mercedes had built the best. Drivers Lewis Hamilton and Nico Rosberg would have made it five 1–2 finishes from the first five races had Lewis Hamilton's power unit not failed in Australia. It was a complete turn-around for Red Bull, the team that had won the last nine races of 2013. Christian Horner was quick to call for an engine equalization process, a call derided by the team principals with a Mercedes engine.

'We went to see Carlos Ghosn,' recalls Newey, 'then the boss of Renault, to put pressure on him to up the budget and basically ask if he could free up more resources so the engine division could accelerate their programme. Ghosn's reply was, "Well, I have no interest in Formula 1. I'm only in it because my marketing people say I should be."

'I'd taken us away from Ferrari in the first year to Renault. I believed, rightly or wrongly, that if you're in a championship battle, Ferrari would never give us equal equipment. We were stuck with Renault for a huge amount of time. Being in a position where it looked like we couldn't be properly competitive at any visible point in the future was just a very dark tunnel to be in.'

In that state of mind Newey was open to approaches from Ferrari who hadn't won a championship in a decade and were desperate for success. 'I really didn't want to leave. For me, it was a huge career gamble

MOST WINS IN A SEASON

Formula 1 settled into a long run of 16-race seasons, but now that has expanded to 24, the metric for most-wins has gone well off the dial. These are Newey's most successful.

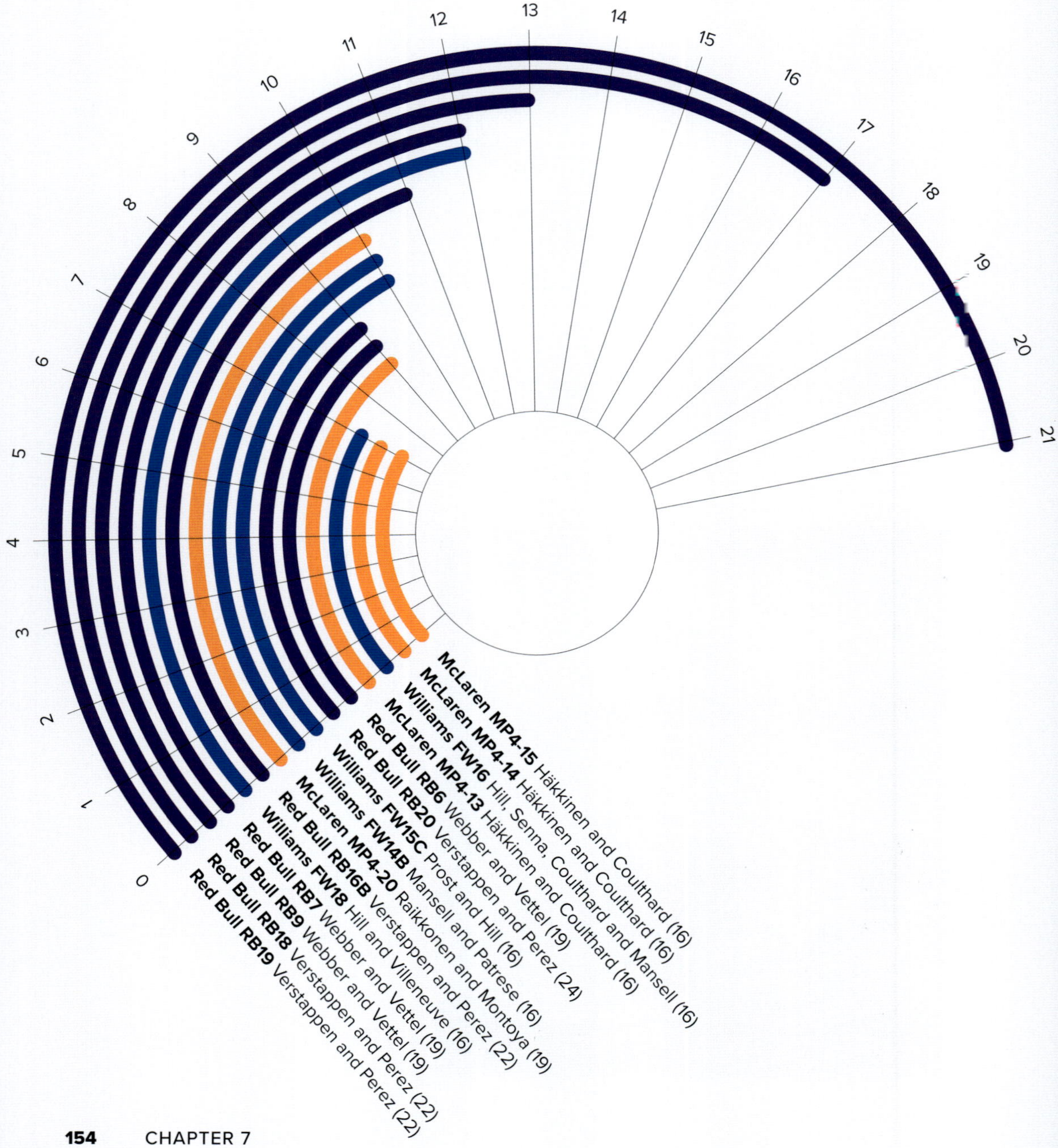

going from McLaren, a championship-winning team, to this start-up, 'jokers of the pit lane' team, but with the ambition obviously of hoping to win a race and maybe even a championship. Then we'd just won four on the trot, which was above our wildest dreams. I was centrally involved and felt almost paternal with the team, in terms of how it developed and the ideas and the effort that we put into it.'

Newey then weighed up (yet again) the disruption moving to Italy would cause, the effect on his children, along with the pressure of the Italian media that always comes with a job at Maranello. He had been offered double his Red Bull salary by Ferrari president Luca di Montezemolo and the chance to join the most iconic of racing teams.

On 8 June 2014, the *Guardian* delivered the verdict: 'Red Bull have seen off a £20m offer from Ferrari to sign up their multi-championship-winning designer Adrian Newey on a fresh long-term contract,' wrote Paul Weaver. 'The new deal will mean Newey stepping back from his day-to-day involvement with the Formula One team and taking on a wider role. As part of this new agreement, Adrian will work on new Red Bull Technology projects, as well as advising and mentoring Infiniti Red Bull Racing as it develops its Formula One cars over the next few seasons.'

Christian Horner, speaking before the Canadian Grand Prix, said: 'It's great we've come to an agreement and that he's going to continue to be advising and mentoring the team going forward. And some exciting new projects will be announced in due course. He will still be very much involved. We've got tremendous strength in depth. It's not like he's not going to be about any more.

'We'll have a further clarification later in the summer. Adrian has reached the stage where he has taken on some additional challenges. It's great news for the team, for Red Bull, that we've got a multi-year agreement. And it's exciting also for Adrian. Hold your breath and we'll talk about that a bit later in the summer.'

After the first five races of 2014 Adrian had spoken his mind to Damien Smith of *Motor Sport* magazine. For a purist such as Newey, grand prix racing had lost its way, however compelling the spectacle might be. Adrian didn't like the quiet, almost Formula E-like noise from the cars and the limited scope for any designer to make a difference.

'There have been a whole host of factors playing their parts in my decision to leave F1,' he told the magazine (prematurely, as it turned out), 'and a lot of mixed emotions. I felt it was time to challenge myself in something different and that's certainly a factor. But at the same time I do think the regs have become too restrictive. We're in danger, chassis-wise, of becoming GP1. Everybody's converging on cars that look more and more similar. We're back to "paint the cars white and it's difficult to spot the difference" – especially next year when we even lose the different noses.'

The Long Return

Horner had persuaded his star designer not to put aside his F1 duties entirely, the RB10, RB11 and RB12 of 2014 to 2016 are Newey-designed cars, but with less of the fine-tuning that Adrian traditionally devoted to his creations. The projects that Horner alluded to were working with the British America's Cup yachting team, a return to the interest he'd professed while at McLaren, and building his first hypercar.

BELOW: Daniil Kvyat at the wheel of the Red Bull RB11 in practice for the 2015 Austrian Grand Prix. Kvyat slotted into the seat left vacant by Sebastian Vettel after his move to Ferrari.

That was a project idea nurtured since his final year at university. Newey believed that the new generation of sports cars were too 'big, heavy and clumsy'. That chimed in with his former schoolmate's view of the Jaguar 220 which was, 'a bit of a labrador – yes it was fast but it handled and braked like a truck', wrote Jeremy Clarkson. Newey was going to break that mould.

Despite the arms'-length approach to the cars of the hybrid engine era, the RB10 in the hands of the team's new Aussie star, Daniel Ricciardo, won three races in 2014. Ricciardo, who had served his apprenticeship at Toro Rosso, eclipsed World Champion Sebastian Vettel, who failed to win a race.

At the Japanese Grand Prix in October Sebastian shocked the paddock by announcing he was leaving to join Ferrari in 2015. His idol Michael Schumacher had gone to Ferrari when the team were in a state of disarray in the mid-1990s and led them to the 'dream team' era of dominance from 2000 to 2004. Vettel had one eye on doing the same, along, of course, with a considerable salary.

'I think you need to understand that there's nothing negative in the air at all,' Sebastian explained to reporters. 'It's not like I'm leaving because I don't like it here or don't like the people any more.' Career-wise it was a sensible move: two seasons of being outscored by his likable team-mate might well have reduced his salary expectations.

Unsurprisingly for an intelligent and thoughtful driver, Vettel certainly did not approach it lightly when he told Horner he would be leaving. Asked if Vettel had been in tears, Horner replied: 'Yes full, full emotion,' he said. 'He was extremely emotional, very emotional. He said it was the hardest thing he had had to do.'

Perhaps manifesting the distractions throughout 2014, the RB11 of 2015 failed to win a single race and didn't even get onto the podium until the Hungarian Grand Prix in late July. It was the first season without a victory since 2009. Owner Dietrich Mateschitz was not happy – earlier in the year Helmut Marko relayed to the paddock his boss's opinion that unless the team could find a competitive engine then they might pull the plug on their F1 operations. This brought a stinging rebuke from the doyen of motorsport writers, Nigel Roebuck.

In the past the 'thoroughbred racer' teams of Williams had endured a torrid time with Judd engines, and McLaren had saddled themselves with Peugeot engines, but neither threatened to walk away from the sport. 'In the hybrid power unit era Renault have undeniably struggled,' he wrote, 'but such was the inherent ability of Newey's RB10 in 2014 that, despite a shortage of power, Ricciardo was still able to win three races. This year the team has gone into free fall, Renault short on power, reliability and driveability, and – with Adrian still involved, but a step removed – Red Bull quite often humbled by its poor relation, Toro Rosso.

'All of this, though, has been compounded by its extraordinary public vilification of its engine partner. Messrs Horner and Marko have gone on at length about the shortcomings of Renault, and clearly this is the company's official policy, for periodically Mateschitz himself weighs in, most recently before the Austrian Grand Prix at the Red Bull Ring. Well, boo bloody hoo. There wasn't much enjoyment for everyone else when Mateschitz's team won nine on the trot in the second half of 2013.'

Martin Brundle believed in the threat from Red Bull's owner, suggesting that the Austrian billionaire wouldn't make such public comments lightly. 'Dietrich Mateschitz is quite publicity-shy, he doesn't say too much and when he does, he doesn't just say things for effect or just because he wants to.'

BELOW: Daniil Kvyat tests the RB12 at the Circuit de Catalunya in February 2016. Two months (and four races) later he would be demoted to the Toro Rosso team

BELOW RIGHT: Max Verstappen made an immediate impact in 2016, winning his debut race after Red Bull split their strategies in Spain.

Verstappen

Walking away from F1 would have meant failing to embrace the potential of two bright new stars coming through the Red Bull Driver Programme in 2015. Carlos Sainz had been a genuine product of Helmut Marko's staircase of driver talent, whereas Max Verstappen was a last-minute addition. Both were installed at Toro Rosso in the 2015 season, with the 17-year-old Verstappen outperforming his slightly more experienced team-mate.

Though often billed as a 'product' of Marko's driver scheme, in truth Verstappen had only signed for Red Bull with five race weekends left of the 2014 European F3 season. After stellar drives at Spa and the Norisring, Marko realised that the only way he could convince Jos Verstappen to sign his boy was to offer him a Toro Rosso seat in 2015. At the time, Toto Wolff was on the brink of getting Max's signature (actually, Jos and mum/former karting champion, Sophie Kumpen), but proposed to run him in GP2 for 2015. Jos, with his eyes on the bigger prize, opted for the race seat.

The sabre-rattling may have worked. The 2016 Renault engine emerged with a TAG-Heuer badge as the watch company took over the naming rights. Adrian was slightly more optimistic about their prospects. 'The gap to the top is still significant, but (at Renault) there are new people, more budget, a different approach, and all that should help us to close the gap slowly but surely. We are in the third year of these regulations, which I think are quite restrictive,' he said. 'So I do not expect a huge step forward.'

Ultimately they scored two race wins in 2016, which turned out to be another Mercedes-dominated year, both coming when the leading Silver Arrows had exited the race. The most exciting win fell to debutant Max Verstappen in Spain after he had been parachuted into the team. Red Bull driver Daniil Kvyat had earned himself

'The Torpedo' nickname and at the fourth race of the season in Sochi had comprehensively taken out Sebastian Vettel's Ferrari. It resulted in one of the all-time-greatest team radio rants from the German driver along with Verstappen's elevation to the senior team at the age of 18 in Kvyat's place.

In the race, polesitter Nico Rosberg failed to select the correct engine mode on the grid. Coming through Turn 3, the closely following Lewis Hamilton realised his team-mate was slow, went for a move on the inside and Rosberg swerved and took them both out. That left a strategy battle between Red Bull and Ferrari – Vettel vs Ricciardo, Räikkönen vs Verstappen; Seb and Daniel on a three-stop strategy (which Red Bull computed to be fastest), Max and Kimi going longer on a two-stop strategy. It was a day when the two-stop strategy worked out and Verstappen resisted an incredible amount of pressure from Räikkönen to finish 0.6 seconds ahead.

In the process Max had broken many of 'F1's youngest ever ...' records: the youngest race winner at 18 years and 228 days, youngest to lead a race, youngest podium appearance – most of which had been held by Sebastian Vettel. There was little doubt that, given a competitive car, there would be a World Championship somewhere down the line. As it was, Red Bull were the only non-Mercedes team to win a race in 2016 and finished second in the constructors' championship, a full 70 points in front of Ferrari.

Losing Ricciardo

Nothing looked like stopping the Mercedes juggernaut in 2017 despite a big change in the technical regulations. In the wake of Mercedes' engine superiority, power unit development had been restricted using a token system. Now a set of regulations were brought in to speed up the machinery. Overall width of the car was increased from 1.8m to 2.m, bodywork width increased from 1.4m to 1.6m, the front-wing width increased, the rear wing lowered and moved backwards by 20cm. The rear diffuser

BELOW LEFT: Daniel Ricciardo in qualifying for the 2017 US Grand Prix at Austin.

RIGHT: Ricciardo scored yet another Red Bull Monaco win in 2018, but it would prove to be his final podium for the team.

height was increased from 125 to 175mm, the leading edge of the barge boards was brought forward to allow teams more freedom in controlling airflow. Tyre width increased by 25 per cent to allow cars to generate more mechanical grip. It was an array of technical freedoms that presented a designer of Newey's ability the opportunity to create a Mercedes challenger. Except Adrian had delegated most of the design and testing of the RB13 to the in-house team while he worked on the Aston Martin hypercar project.

After just a couple of podiums it became clear that the 2017 car was not the breakthrough they had hoped for. Newey was called in to attend the Spanish Grand Prix where Christian Horner fielded questions from the press about the superstar designer's effectiveness. 'Adrian has been listening very carefully to what the drivers have been saying and it is a bit like a trip to the doctors. He has been very keen to understand what the drivers' feedback and comments are, and I am sure he will be looking to evolve this package accordingly,' was the response. Horner made clear that Adrian's F1 involvement was at least 50 per cent of his workload. 'He has sat in the weekly meetings. He has been very involved in this development of the car and the concept of this car. The design group is structured to accommodate the way that Adrian works in a fairly unique manner.'

'I had stepped right back, but it became obvious that the car under a more delegated, or a committee way of operating, wasn't performing,' Newey told *Autosport*. 'As a kind of a duty to the team, to try and bring things forward, I have been quite busy since the second test, getting back involved to see what I can do to help.

'It's not what I want to be doing long term, but I'm happy to be doing it for a period of time. I think what's clear is that my stepping back in a system of regulatory stability, then the system was working, but that kind of committee approach hasn't worked when we've had a big regulation change.'

Things got a little testy as to why Adrian hadn't brought his A-game to the 2017 car. Was it the process Christian had put in place or down to Newey's failure to bring his out-of-the-box thinking to the RB13?

'He's regularly sitting with the technical principals,' said Horner defensively. 'I think communication across the departments is possibly what he's referring to. Perhaps he hasn't followed the regulation changes as he would have done previously. So now he's trying to bring himself up to speed as well.'

In the end, Red Bull scored three wins in 2017 to finish third in the constructors' table behind a resurgent Ferrari. A glance much further down the table would find his former employer, McLaren, in a lowly ninth position. If Newey thought his Renault engine was underpowered, then the unreliable Honda hybrid engine that

BELOW: The 2018 Azerbaijan Grand Prix proved to be the flashpoint in Ricciardo's relationship with the team – feeling that his team-mate had shrugged off any blame for an accident that cost the team a 1–2 result.

BELOW RIGHT: Max Verstappen in practice for the 2019 Austrian Grand Prix, the team's first season equipped with Honda engines.

McLaren had so handsomely welcomed in 2015 had been a complete and utter disaster. The Japanese engine giant had totally underestimated the challenge of the hybrid engine and were reportedly a year behind Mercedes, Ferrari and Renault. There were many design glitches to rectify, but the biggest problem was it could not harvest enough energy to deploy along the entire length of all but the shortest of straights. It meant that Alonso, Button and subsequently Vandoorne ran out of hybrid power – an immediate loss of at least 160bhp – part-way along straights. Alonso became very vocal about the Honda engine performance in response.

McLaren and Honda parted company at the end of the 2017 season and Toro Rosso took the engine supply the following year. Honda's 2018 power unit, the RA618H, was a more mature variant of the engine architecture introduced in 2017, while Toro Rosso enjoyed significantly greater reliability compared to that experienced by McLaren. And in just the second race of the season, Bahrain, Pierre Gasly brought his Toro Rosso home in fourth place.

The attitude of the Honda engine team and their constant striving to improve – introducing Spec 2 and Spec 3 through the course of the season – impressed the

Red Bull management. They committed to Honda for the senior team in 2019, even though estimates had the engine as 30bhp down on the Renault, and even more to Mercedes and Ferrari.

Their own 2018 season was a step up in that they scored four victories compared to the previous season's three – and it should have been five. Daniel Ricciardo had won the third race in China and celebrated with his trademark 'Shoey' – an act so compelling that Liberty Media trademarked the term for a champagne-in-boot celebration moment.

The following race was Azerbaijan where Ricciardo had won in 2017. On Lap 40 the two Red Bulls were running line astern in fourth and fifth place – Verstappen having just passed Ricciardo in the tyre stops. Daniel went for an overtaking move into Turn 1, Max moved to the outside to block him; when Daniel switched back to the inside, Verstappen moved back to block him for a second time, brakes were locked and Ricciardo slammed into the back of his team-mate. Both cars were out on the spot.

To the rest of the world it looked like Verstappen's fault, to Helmut Marko it was Ricciardo's fault – Daniel took note of the lack of any sanction on the Dutchman – 'he just kinda shrugged his shoulders', fully aware of what had happened to his Aussie predecessor. Two races later he won the Monaco Grand Prix having set a new qualifying lap record to take pole position. Verstappen had put his car into the barriers in FP3 and his mechanics couldn't rebuild it in time. Thus Red Bull started the most important race for their sponsor TAG-Heuer in first and last place. The entire pit lane was convinced Ricciardo would stay on with Red Bull for 2019–2020 but chose the 'new challenge' of Renault. Christian Horner was so surprised by his decision to join Renault that when Daniel phoned him to tell him the news he thought he was joking.

Honda impress

After 12 years together Adrian Newey described Red Bull's relationship with Renault as a 'broken marriage'. There had been constant bickering for the last three years and now it was divorce. For the team's principal asset, the new engine supply couldn't come soon enough. 'Honda are really a breath of fresh air,' Adrian told Sky Sports, 'They are great people to work with, very straightforward,

LEFT: Max Verstappen points to his engine badge after the 2019 Austrian win. It was a tremendous morale boost for the Honda engineers and Newey was well aware that they would not hold back on refining the engine further.

RIGHT: Daniel Ricciardo's replacement was Toro Rosso's Pierre Gasly who threw himself into all the promotions that Red Bull lined up. At Silverstone, sponsor Aston Martin organised an 007 DB5 for a photo opportunity. Gasly may have been driving, but in reality he was in the ejector seat.

very well organised. It's actually motivated the whole team having this new relationship with them. They're not quite at Mercedes or Ferrari level yet, but I have every confidence that they will get there quite quickly. They just instil that confidence.'

Along with a new engine came a new driver: Pierre Gasly was promoted from Toro Rosso to take on the challenge of partnering Max Verstappen.

Newey was honest about his own contribution: 'On the chassis side, I'll be brutally honest, we haven't got the car as good as we'd like it to be at the moment. We just need to get on and do our bit.'

He was asked why he had stayed at Red Bull for 13 years. 'I just feel very comfortable. I enjoy working with the people there and because Christian and I have been responsible for shaping how it is today, then why would I want to leave?'

Though the RB15 of 2019 was never going to win either title, with perfect timing the highlight of the year came at the Austrian Grand Prix at the Red Bull Ring in late June. Max Verstappen started the race from P3 but encountered an issue with his anti-stall, dropping from second down to eighth place by Turn 1. The Oranje Army filling the grandstands were silent. It looked like this was going to be a bogey weekend after Max had destroyed his car in free practice, losing control out of the final turn.

But in that glitch lay his salvation. Ferrari, with Leclerc on pole, immediately switched their attention to counter the strategy run by the Mercedes' front-runner Valtteri Bottas, while Verstappen ran a long first stint. As the race closed out, Max, on fresher tyres, drove thrillingly, overhauling second-place Bottas on Lap 56

(of 71). He reached leader Leclerc and made a controversial passing move on Lap 69, making contact with the Ferrari and pushing him over the kerbs. The stewards deemed it legal, much to Leclerc's indignation.

As Max stood on the podium he yanked the Honda badge of his overalls and pointed to the Japanese engineers below. They were in tears. Verstappen's victory marked the first win for a Honda-powered F1 car since Jenson Button at the 2006 Hungarian Grand Prix. They had poured resources into the engine project after the McLaren debacle – using the HondaJet Divison to rectify failures on the MGU-H and the turbo-charger, bringing in more English-speaking engineers and

ABOVE: The grid for the 2020 Austrian Grand Prix, run with no spectators under the enforced Covid 19 protocols.

aggressively developing the power unit at every opportunity. This was the attitude that Newey found so motivating – and now the Japanese company had got their just reward in the hands of F1's record-breaking driver.

But whereas Ricciardo and Verstappen had shared the wins in 2018, all three would go to Max in 2019. The under-performing Pierre Gasly was deemed unable to take the pressure in the top team and was replaced by Alex Albon mid-season in a continuation of Red Bull's revolving door policy for its drivers. Honda got their second and third wins in Germany and Brazil and the team finished their first season with a new power unit placing third. That may have been the same result as 2018, but now the trajectory was up.

Given their engine partner's enthusiasm and investment, the 2020 season promised to be a year when Red Bull challenged at the front again. The global Covid pandemic which struck on the eve of the Australian Grand Prix in Melbourne knocked everyone off balance. There were also problems with the chassis, which Adrian Newey revealed in 2021. 'When we moved from the RB15 of 2019 to the RB16 of 2020, there were some things on the car that we didn't fully understand,' he told a Red Bull podcast. 'Even with the wind tunnel programme and all of our simulation tools there are still things that can trip you up, and that's exactly what happened at the start of 2020.

'It took a bit of time to understand and get on top of those issues. The benefit of that – as is often the case – is that you learn things that you wouldn't otherwise have learned. Sometimes you get more out of the mistakes than you do the good things.'

As the world came to terms with the impositions of a global lockdown in 2020, the seven UK F1 teams combined their engineering experience to create respirators termed 'Project Pitlane'. The season would eventually get under way in July with an Austrian double-header, a single race in Hungary and another double-header at Silverstone, all run under tight pandemic protocols with team members in their own respective bubbles.

So often the recipient of other teams' rule challenges to their technical innovation, in 2020 it was Newey's Red Bull who tried to get a rival team's idea banned. Ahead of the season-opening grand prix, Red Bull launched a protest against the Mercedes W11's dual axis steering, a system where the driver can adjust the toe angle of the wheels by pulling and pushing on the steering wheel. The system was found to be legal for 2020, but it would be banned by the FIA from 2021 onwards.

It was another step on the learning curve for Red Bull as most of the teams adapted to a truncated season. What was clear from a driver perspective was that Alex Albon could not match his rapidly maturing team-mate, now in his sixth season on the grid. Albon finished the season with two podiums while Max took two wins and 11 podiums. What was worse, Pierre Gasly, relegated to the Toro Rosso team, managed to win the Italian Grand Prix. Should he be re-promoted to Red Bull ...?

2021: F1 gets fraught

In a late-December announcement Christian Horner revealed that: 'Having taken our time to evaluate all the relevant data and performances we have decided that Sergio [Perez] is the right driver to partner Max for 2021.' In what was rapidly becoming a tyre management formula, Perez's acknowledged ability to make his Pirellis last beyond their best was viewed as a considerable advantage if Red Bull wanted to claim the constructors' title. They had already inched up the table to second place in 2020.

Coming into the 2021 season, and aware that finances in all the F1 teams would be tight, the FIA had implemented a $145m budget cap. They also mandated that teams should carry over their 2020 chassis, limiting major areas of change by the use of 'development tokens'. Some parts of the car could be changed token-free, for example the power unit, the cooling systems, the suspension and all of the aerodynamic surfaces. That didn't include the gearbox. Teams had to nominate the areas they would develop on their 2021 cars by June 2020, effectively sealing in their development plans.

Five days after the homologation plans were accepted, the FIA wrote to teams informing them of a further step in aero regulation changes for 2021 to cut back on downforce. This included greater restrictions on the floor dimensions, plus changes to the lower bargeboard area. These changes would affect the low-rake cars

BELOW RIGHT: Verstappen pulls up and salutes the grandstand at the Red Bull Ring having won his fifth race of 2021.

BELOW: Given the inability of the Red Bull Driver Programme to provide a suitable team-mate for Max Verstappen, the team drafted in the experienced (and tyre friendly) Sergio Perez in 2021.

(Mercedes) far more than the high-rake models (Red Bull). The most obvious solution would have been for Mercedes to alter its gearbox to help it raise the rear ride height to overcome the consequences. Except they hadn't nominated a gearbox token in their development plan and so it was a route they now couldn't pursue. Mercedes sensed this sudden announcement, coming just days after the development token deadline, was aimed at reeling them in – they had won 15 races out of 21 the previous year.

The tumultuous 2021 season started off on a positive note for the Milton Keynes team, Newey describing the RB16B as 'a decent step forwards. It seems we read the regulation changes on the aerodynamics reasonably well' he told the *Raging Bulls* podcast. They had also made wise choices for their development

tokens. 'I can't remember this happening before, this homologation of the previous year's car into the next season. It meant we were very limited on what we could do to the car. We decided to spend those [tokens] on the gearbox casing and that allowed us to also change the rear suspension arrangements, which was one thing I didn't feel had worked that well on the RB16.'

Red Bull looked strong in pre-season testing to the surprise of many, but Newey remained cautious. 'Coming out of the Bahrain testing, we felt we had a competitive package. But of course, you never know where exactly that's going to be. You don't know what engine modes people are running, what fuel loads, and so on and so forth.'

ABOVE AND BELOW RIGHT: Two images from the resurrected Dutch Grand Prix in 2021. Max prepares to launch himself down the main straight, which was initially built during World War II as a 'paradestrasse' and on the distinctive Zandvoort banking.

ABOVE RIGHT: A shaken Max climbs from his car in the run-off to Copse corner at the 2021 British Grand Prix.

From race one, they were super-competitive. Verstappen and Hamilton finished 1–2 in six of the first eight races, Lewis winning three and Max winning three. When Verstappen won in Austria (scoring his first career grand slam of pole, fastest lap, win, and leading every lap of the race) Hamilton failed to get on the podium. As they headed for Silverstone, Max had a 32-point lead in the championship and after a win in the Sprint race, every chance of widening the gap further. The main grand prix was described by the BBC's Andrew Benson as 'a seismic moment in the 2021 Formula 1 title battle, featuring an incident that will become a defining part of the sport's history. The two championship contenders collided, resulting in a high-speed crash at Copse corner for one of them and a brilliant if controversial victory by the other, and rancour and recriminations afterwards.'

The accident on the opening lap left Adrian Newey 'incandescent' with rage. 'I felt it was a deliberate professional foul,' he told the *High Performance* podcast. 'I think now, with the benefit of hindsight and time ... there'd been banging wheels all the way around the lap up to that corner.' Christian Horner was outspoken about the incident and called Hamilton 'a dirty driver', it was a 'desperate move' and 'an amateur mistake'.

'I got a great tow down to Copse,' Hamilton revealed. 'Yesterday, [in the sprint] I went down the left and really regretted not going for the gap that was on the right-hand side. So I dummied him, moved to the left and then moved to the

COURSE
Mobil
citrix
RedBull

HONDA
Claro
ESSO
HONDA
ORACLE
telcel
Mobil 1

right for that gap. I was pretty far alongside him but I could see he wasn't going to back out. Then we went into the corner and we collided.'

'Hamilton had the majority of his car alongside Verstappen's as they turned in,' Benson wrote, 'but the Red Bull driver had squeezed him tight to the inside before moving back towards the left, so Hamilton was approaching Copse at a shallow angle.'

Realising that Verstappen was not going to give him room, Hamilton backed out at the last minute. It was too late. The Red Bull was sent hurtling towards the barriers and thankfully Verstappen walked away from the car. The stewards judged Hamilton to be 'predominantly at fault' for the accident. Even so he made two further overtakes at Copse – on Norris and Leclerc – without incident. Ferrari's Charles Leclerc, who had been following the pair said: 'It is a racing incident. It is quite difficult to put the blame on one or the other. There was space on the inside. Maybe Lewis was not completely at the apex but it is also true Max was quite aggressive on the outside.'

Fernando Alonso agreed: 'Lewis had more than half a car alongside Max, so in a way Lewis could not disappear from that inside line. You can't vanish. So it

BELOW: Verstappen's late lunge on Hamilton in the 2021 Italian Grand Prix ended with the rear tyre of his RB16B impacting Lewis's helmet.

was an unfortunate moment but nothing intentional and nothing that any of the two drivers did wrong.'

Some years later Newey's view on the incident had mellowed. 'We were lucky that Max didn't get hurt badly in that accident. I was probably a bit too harsh on Lewis at the time. And that's perhaps one of the things of Formula 1, you get sucked into everybody else being the enemy very easily.'

It set the tone for the rest of the season. When Red Bull made an unusually slow pit stop at the Italian Grand Prix, Verstappen was released behind Hamilton. Hammering into the first chicane at Monza, the Rettifilo, Max attempted the kind of optimistic lunge more typical of GP3 than F1. His Red Bull mounted the kerb and launched across the back of the Silver Arrows car with his rear tyre clattering down partly onto Hamilton's helmet, with the halo taking the bulk of the weight. Both cars out on the spot, Hamilton mercifully uninjured by the tyre impact.

In Brazil, four races from the end of the season, there was speculation that Red Bull had got wind that the DRS slot gap on the Mercedes was (favourably) too wide. After Lewis Hamilton had claimed pole by 0.4 of a second, the cars were assembled in *parc fermé* when Max Verstappen walked over and, inexplicably, touched the DRS flap on the rear wing of the Mercedes car – an illegal act for which he was later fined €50,000. Red Bull then protested about the size of the slot gap, which was found to be correct in the centre, but 0.2mm too wide at the outer edges. Hamilton was disqualified and sent to the back of the grid for sprin qualifying. He still won the race, despite being forced off the road at Turn 4, Lake Descent, in a Max Verstappen move that would be a future reference point about what is and what is not allowed when overtaking on the outside.

There were allegations of brake-testing in Saudi Arabia before the final climax at Yas Marina in Abu Dhabi. Hamilton led the race and was destined for victory and his eighth World Championship as cars circulated behind the safety car following a late-race Nicholas Latifi crash. FIA race director Michael Masi should have then released the lapped cars between leader Hamilton (on worn tyres) and second-place Verstappen (on new tyres) to rejoin at the back of the pack. But the process would have taken too long and the final lap was approaching. Instead, he green-flagged the race and on fresher tyres let Verstappen loose to claim the race win and his first drivers' title.

In world sport it is hard to think of a mistake that is so grave but remains uncorrected. It was jubilation for Red Bull in the bitter fight against Mercedes. Lewis Hamilton to his eternal credit was a gracious, if slightly shell-shocked loser.

However, nobody thought that Verstappen was an unworthy World Champion. For Adrian Newey it was perhaps something the FIA owed him. All through his career his innovation and technical prowess had been stymied by FIA dictats when rival teams (most commonly Ferrari) had objected because of their ingenuity. In 1999 at McLaren he had certainly lost a constructors' title thanks to direct FIA intervention in the bargeboard fiasco. This was the FIA finally handing something back. If things felt good on the evening of 12 December 2021, they were just about to get even better.

2022: A New Era

The strict rules on chassis design introduced for the 2022 season had originally been intended for 2021, but then Covid 19 arrived and pushed them back a season. They were intended to create more overtaking action – cars under the existing regulations could not get close enough in the dirty air created by the aero package of the car in front. A research group estimated that cars lost 35 per cent of their downforce within three car lengths when following and almost 50 per cent in a single car length. The new, more prescriptive aero package aimed to reduce those numbers to 4 and 18 per cent respectively.

Given Adrian's long-held irritation with the tight strictures of modern regulations, one might have assumed that he had little room for manoeuvre. Except ... the proposed way of recovering the downforce lost by 'cleaning up' the wake from the 2022 cars was a return to ground effect. The new cars would be allowed two Venturi tunnels through the floor. The self-effacing 63-year-old often called himself 'an old dinosaur' for using a drawing board when the world had moved on to Computer Aided Design (CAD), but he was the only designer working in F1 with first-hand experience of ground effect F1 cars.

Newey welcomed the challenge. 'I would say this is the biggest single regulation change we've had since the ground effect cars were banned at the end of 1982. It really is a revolution. The only thing that stays the same is the power unit, everything else is different.'

But there was a balancing act to be done. The title fight of 2021 meant the Red Bull team were engaged in developing the RB16B until the end of the season instead of working on its revolutionary successor the RB18. Ferrari had switched resources to their 2022 challenger, the F1-75, far earlier.

'We kept developing for longer than either Ferrari or Mercedes, so theoretically that put us at a disadvantage. I think what we did manage to do is

RIGHT: Max takes the outside line into Turn 1 at Suzuka in the 2022 Japanese GP to pass Charles Leclerc. The race was stopped short but full points were awarded, making a surprised Max champion.

BELOW: Max Verstappen streaks away at the start of the 2022 Mexican Grand Prix. It would be his 14th victory (of 15) that year.

get the architecture right. When RB18 first came out in Bahrain, the Ferrari was certainly as quick, if not quicker in the early season, but we managed to get the fundamentals right and that gave us a good development platform.'

The early races of 2022 gave great hope to Ferrari's *tifosi*. The team had struggled to regain form after the FIA caught them gaming the engine fuel sensor in 2019 and had gone rapidly backwards – as Max Verstappen observed to the Scuderia's fury at the time: 'That's what happens when you stop cheating'.

After the first three races of the season, Charles Leclerc held a 46-point lead over Verstappen, who had retired from both the opening race in Bahrain and the third race in Australia. Max, now with No.1 on his car, was beginning to get agitated. He *had* won the intervening race in Saudi Arabia and the old motorsport adage is true: it's easier to make a fast car reliable than make a reliable car fast. Starting with victory at Imola he reeled off wins in Miami, Barcelona, Monaco, Baku and Montreal.

At Silverstone and the Red Bull Ring he had to concede victory to Ferrari, but then he put together another nine straight GP wins matching Sebastian Vettel's

RIGHT: Max Verstappen at the Azerbaijan Grand Prix of 2023, a race that he lost to Sergio Perez, but where he unlocked the set-up secrets of the RB19.

BELOW: The G.O.A.T. of F1 cars: Sergio Perez in the RB19 during sprint shoot-out qualifying for the 2023 Brazilian Grand Prix at Interlagos.

winning sequence of 2013. The drivers' title came his way four races before the end of the season, in a curtailed Japanese Grand Prix. This time Red Bull picked up both trophies, Newey's Honda-powered RB18 finishing more than 200 points ahead of Ferrari.

2023: The Ultimate

The logic of any F1 rules re-set is that the following season, teams will have learned from their mistakes – and the development path of the Mercedes W13 had been a big one – while copying all the best elements of rival cars.

Heading into 2023 there was much anticipation that both Ferrari and particularly Mercedes, with the ever-improving George Russell, would come back far stronger. This viewpoint, however, didn't factor in the knowledge that the RB18 had been rushed through. Adrian Newey still had speed to add to the car. Max Verstappen would go on to thank the team for providing him with a 'rocket ship', the RB19.

'Weight loss was part of the RB19's success,' Newey told the BBC's Andrew Benson. 'We never managed to get down to the weight limit in 2022. By the end of the season, we were still significantly over, so much more detail through the winter to get the weight off.

'It's all about trying to condition the airflow to give the best performance to the underbody. Most of what you see is as always to control the front-wheel wake, which in any open-wheel racing car is a big thing, and maximising the shape of the floor is the key to the whole thing.'

Newey's ability to stop the car from bouncing or porpoising in the first two years of the new rules was envied across the grid – the low pressure sucks the car down, but when the car gets low enough, the airflow can become disrupted, and

LEFT: A compilation of podium shots showing Max Verstappen's ten successive wins (including a rain-soaked Zandvoort full of jeopardy) in 2023. It was ample evidence of the RB19's dominance.

RIGHT: Having missed out under the lights of Singapore in 2023, Max was in no mood to give best to Charles Leclerc under the brighter lights of Las Vegas.

the car jumps up, only for the airflow to start working again, sucking the car down again before the process repeats.

'I was surprised that nobody really saw that coming, to be perfectly honest, because it was certainly a problem in the 1980s. With those ground effect cars in 1981 we decided that because we were running the front so stiff, we could save weight by throwing away the springs and dampers and just substituting them with a bump rubber. We took that solution up to Silverstone for a test and Keke Rosberg was driving the car, and as it came past the pits, it was bouncing so badly that you could see daylight under the front tyres. That was a lesson in how badly you could get it wrong.'

Even after two years of the new rules Adrian was still reluctant to disclose exactly where the car's advantage lay – although competitors would get a very good view of the RB20 floor when Perez collided with Magnusson on the first lap of the 2024 Monaco GP and his car was hoisted high above the grandstands.

Speaking to Tom Clarkson about the success of the RB19, Newey was still coy about the elements that he had exploited to create such an all-conquering car. 'Formula 1's a very secretive business. Some people liken it to warfare, we're all competing with each other, and we're desperately trying to hang on to our intellectual property which other teams don't copy or understand. The bits that I feel some teams may not have still fully understood, I therefore don't really feel it's appropriate to talk about.'

The RB19 turned out to be F1's most dominant car, winning the biggest tally of races in any single season, 21 of the 22 grands prix – 19 to Verstappen, two to

Perez. The only blip on the perfect score was the Singapore GP where Carlos Sainz won a tactical masterclass keeping Lando Norris in DRS range to provide a buffer between himself and the faster Mercedes of George Russell.

At the start of the year Verstappen and Perez had shared the first four grand prix victories. The fourth race had been on the streets of Baku where Max followed Checo for lap after lap. Having tangled with Ricciardo in the past, and crashed out with a tyre failure in Azerbaijan in 2021, Max decided to treat the second half of the race as a practice session.

Helmut Marko and Adrian are agreed that Verstappen's genius stems partly from his ability to compute so many things at once. While other drivers need all their focus to keep the car on the island and stop their tyres wearing out, Max has 'mental reserve' left over. Following his team-mate around Baku he started playing around with different set-ups on his steering wheel and at the end he told father Jos, 'I think I've found it now, what we need to do.'

Perez was on pole for the next race in Miami after a Q3 red flag left Max in ninth unable to improve his time. In the race, Verstappen thundered through the field to take the win. Helmut Marko was typically brutal about Perez's subsequent dismal performances. 'He has now woken up from his World Championship dream. Maybe that will help him to focus again on delivering the best possible

BELOW LEFT: The senior team at Red Bull had every reason to celebrate 2023 when F1 milestones were torn out of the ground. Raymond Vermeulen (Max's manager) waits for his driver along with Helmut Marko, Christian Horner and Adrian Newey.

BELOW RIGHT: The Bahrain Grand Prix of 2024 would prove to be a routine 1-2 for the Red Bull team with Newey's RB20 off to a winning start. Behind the scenes it was far from business as usual.

performance.' Verstappen went on to eclipse his shared 2022 record with Vettel by winning ten races in a row, the last in front of the *tifosi* at Monza.

Newey was keen to play down the routine-ness of continually winning. 'This has been the biggest success that I've certainly ever experienced. We've been fortunate enough to be involved with cars that have been dominant in the past, but we've never had this level of consistency. People might think now that everything is guaranteed and it'll be smooth and blah, blah, blah. The reality is so many things can go wrong in a race.' Indeed, the Dutch Grand Prix had taken place in a downpour but Verstappen had battled through. 'So many elements that can go wrong; reliability, accidents, strategy, performance, so to achieve this is a real tribute to everybody.'

It had been a year of crushing superiority, with so many milestones passed. At the 2023 Canadian Grand Prix, Verstappen took Red Bull's 100th win (all of the cars designed by Adrian), which also marked Newey's 200th win in Formula 1. Given that level of achievement the paddock and the media were blindsided about what would happen next.

F1'S MOST DOMINANT CARS

Lined up on the grid in percentage of race wins. This includes cars from 1950 when there were just six races to 2023, when there were 22. It also includes cars that raced for more than one season in the 1950s.

WILLIAMS FW14B
10 Wins 1992
62.5%

RED BULL RB9
13 Wins 2013
68.42%

MERCEDES W196
9 Wins 1954/55
75%

FERRARI F2004
15 Wins 2004
75%

RED BULL RB18
17 wins 2022
77.27%

WILLIAMS FW15C
10 Wins 1993
62.5%

BENETTON B195
11 Wins 1995
64.7%

MERCEDES W10
15 Wins 2019
71.43%

WILLIAMS FW18
12 Wins 1996
75%

MERCEDES W11
15 Wins 2020
76.47%

But if that grid was based on the sheer number of wins, this is what it would look like...

MERCEDES W196
1954/55 75%
9 wins

WILLIAMS FW14B
1992 62.5%
10 wins

WILLIAMS FW18
1996 75%
12 wins

RED BULL RB9
2013 68.42%
13 wins

FERRARI F2004
2004 75%
15 wins

ALPHA ROMEO 158
1950 100%
6 wins

WILLIAMS FW15C
1993 62.5%
10 wins

BENETTON B195
1995 64.7%
11 wins

MERCEDES W11
2020 76.47%
15 wins

FERRARI TIPO 500
1952/3 93.33%
14 wins

MERCEDES W05
16 Wins 2014
84.21%

MERCEDES W07
19 Wins 2016
90.48%

MCLAREN MP4/4
15 Wins 1988
93.75%

ALPHA ROMEO 158
6 wins 1950
100%

FERRARI F2002
15 Wins 2002
78.95%

MERCEDES W06
16 Wins 2015
84.21%

FERRARI TIPO 500
14 Wins 1952/3
93.33%

RED BULL RB19
21 wins 2023
95.45%

MCLAREN MP4/4
1988 93.75%
15 wins

MERCEDES W06
2015 84.21%
16 wins

RED BULL RB18
2022 77.27%
17 wins

RED BULL RB19
2023 95.45%
21 wins

MERCEDES W10
2019 71.43%
15 wins

FERRARI F2002
2002 78.95%
15 wins

MERCEDES W05
2014 84.21%
16 wins

MERCEDES W07
2016 90.48%
19 wins

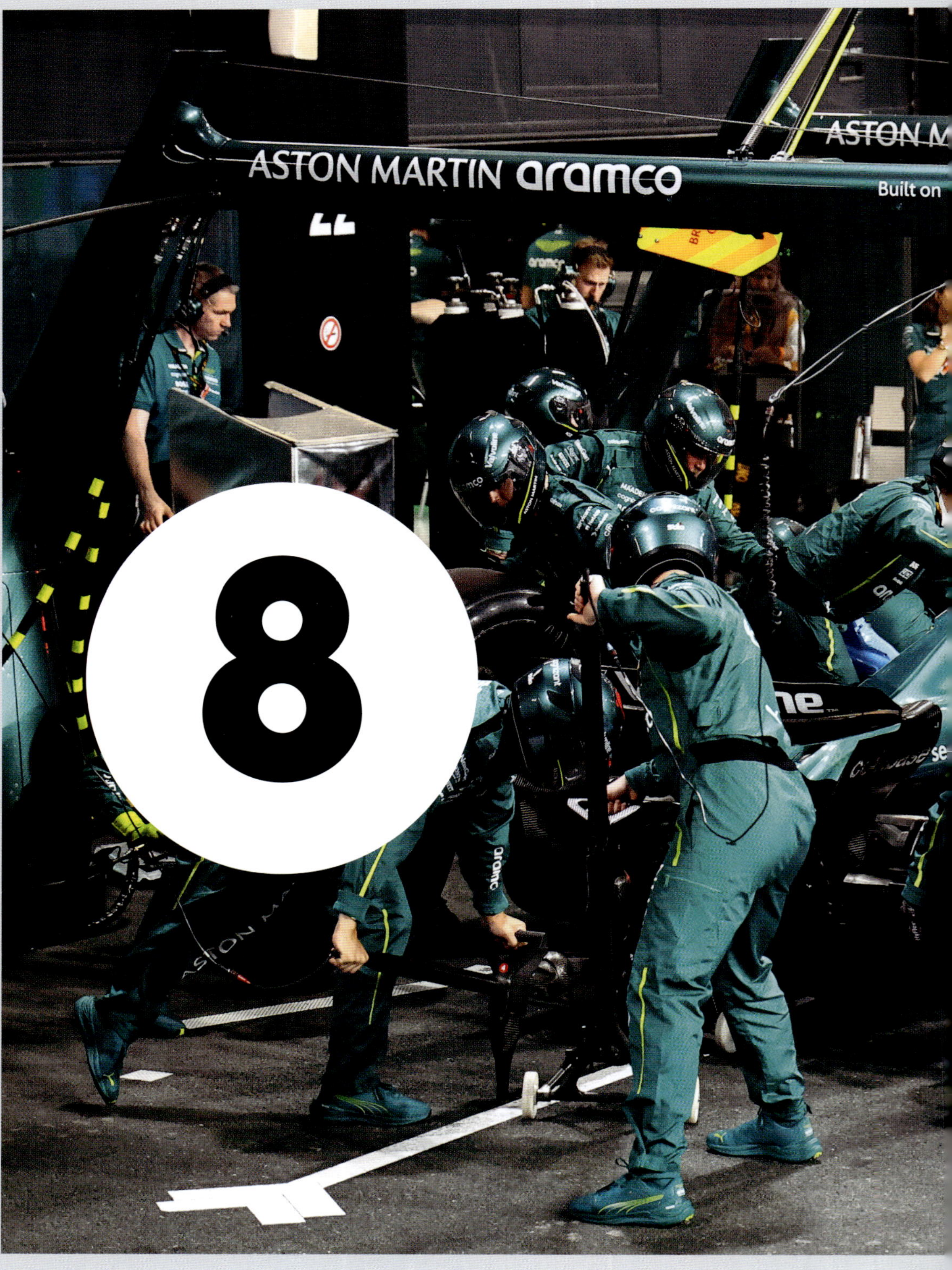

8

aramco
Built on arm
25
aramco

ASTON MARTIN

For the first two races of 2024 it looked like business as usual from the Red Bull team. The evolution of the unbeatable RB19, the RB20, looked strong in testing and a 1–2 in Bahrain followed by a 1–2 in Saudi Arabia gave the paddock the ominous feeling that this might be 2023 all over again.

Behind the scenes, it was far from business as usual. On 2 February, Dutch newspaper *De Telegraaf* revealed that the team had begun an investigation into alleged 'inappropriate behaviour' by team principal Christian Horner with a female employee.

There was no getting away from it at the Red Bull team launch on 15 February. Journalists were instructed not to ask Max Verstappen, Sergio Perez or Horner directly about proceedings but Horner didn't shy away from the subject. 'My focus is very much on the season ahead, it has been business as normal. Obviously there is an investigation that I'm complying with and working with fully. So that is very much going on in the background.'

PREVIOUS PAGE: An Aston Martin pit stop. Anything more than three seconds in modern F1 is seen as under performing.

LEFT: It was a surprise to many when former F1 team boss Eddie Jordan stepped into the fray as Adrian's manager. Apart from the motorsport connection they shared a love of superyachts.

RIGHT: Some brief words for the team prior to the 2024 Miami Grand Prix, Adrian's last race in an official capacity. He would continue as a Red Bull employee handling the last stages of the RB17 hypercar and attending Silverstone.

A few days later *De Telegraaf*, for whom Jos Verstappen is a columnist, reported that Horner offered a settlement of £650,000 to the employee in question. This was never confirmed.

After more than 50 hours of interviews, Red Bull announced the result of their independent enquiry, that no further action would be taken. Then, as the teams assembled for the first round, the Bahrain Grand Prix, a cache of the alleged WhatsApp messages was sent to journalists, the FIA and team bosses from an anonymous source, re-igniting the row.

Lines were being drawn up. On one side Helmut Marko with Jos Verstappen, who publicly questioned Horner's leadership: 'The team is in danger of being torn apart,' said the most influential driver parent. 'It can't go on the way it is. It will

explode. He is playing the victim, when he is the one causing the problems.'

On the other side, Horner, backed by Red Bull co-owner Chalerm Yoovidhya. This did not make for the 'comfortable' work environment Newey was used to. Things had never been quite the same after Dietrich Mateschitz died of pancreatic cancer in October 2022. Now the team was answerable to Oliver Mintzlaff, previously the head of Red Bull Global World Soccer.

LEFT: What might have been ... Adrian exchanges some warm words with Piero Ferrari on the grid at the Miami Grand Prix in 2024.

ABOVE RIGHT: Launching the RB17 hypercar at the Goodwood Festival of Speed in 2024. The event also showcased 20 years of Red Bull in Formula 1 with an impressive line-up of former drivers taking cars up the hill.

On 25 April, BBC Sport broke the news that Adrian Newey was leaving the Red Bull team, a fact confirmed by a company press release on 1 May. He would say his farewells at the Miami Grand Prix on 5 May. The BBC added, 'The British design chief has been strongly linked with Ferrari and is known to have been made an offer by Aston Martin, but he is likely to be of interest to all leading teams now his availability is known.'

Newey's contract with Red Bull ran until the end of 2025, with a year of gardening leave after that, but his manager was confident he could finish sooner. The shock of Newey leaving had almost been as great as Lewis Hamilton's announcement that he was joining Ferrari. What was more intriguing was that Adrian's negotiations had been conducted by former F1 team boss Eddie Jordan. Jordan and Newey both shared a great love of sailing – no surprise if one considers that Newey's career has been all about the movement of air. One of EJ's many post-F1 jobs was as a non-executive director of Oyster yachts in

Southampton and Newey had ordered a bespoke 90-foot Oyster 885. Deal-maker Eddie was now in the perfect position to negotiate for him – should he wish to continue.

The subject of retirement had come up the previous autumn. During a summer holiday in Croatia a few years earlier Adrian was riding a bike back from a restaurant in the dark when he veered off the path and crashed into a rock, suffering a serious head injury. It was rumoured that Bernie Ecclestone had used his contacts to get Newey flown home as soon as possible. Unsurprisingly, Adrian didn't want to make a fuss about the incident but third wife, Amanda Smerczak, celebrated his birthday that year with a post on social media. 'August, I came close to losing the love of my life after his cycling accident. Multiple skull fractures – to then sitting on the virtual pit wall [ie back at Milton Keynes HQ] of the Dutch Grand Prix within ten days of his craniotomy displays his strength and drive. His recovery has been nothing short of miraculous.'

Asked by Andrew Benson if the accident made him re-assess his life, Newey smiled: 'I think I am too pig-headed and stupid to do that. Retirement is a funny thing, isn't it. If you'd asked me when I was 50 if I would still be working now, I would have said: "No, absolutely not".

'And then, of course, things come up, and you think, "I'm actually enjoying it and what else would I do?" I'd get bored lying on a beach. Mandy says I would drive her crazy. Two of the people I most respect are Bernie Ecclestone and Roger Penske, both of whom are still working at quite a ripe old age and are still very mentally agile.

'I asked both of them, what's their secret? And they both said: "Don't stop working. Think of your brain as a muscle that needs exercise." And I do agree with that from other observations. Unfortunately, my father retired at 65, and kind of ended up a little bit lost afterwards, I suppose. I don't think he'd mind me saying that.'

Newey was reflecting before the final race of the 2023 season. Things were about to change.

RIGHT: Lawrence Stroll welcomes Adrian Newey to his team at a press conference held at the Aston Martin factory in Silverstone.

BELOW: Old Reptonian Jeremy Clarkson and Diddly Squat entrepreneur Lisa Hogan on the grid at Silverstone in 2024 with Newey.

BELOW RIGHT: Aston Martin CEO Andy Cowell checks that Adrian's drawing board is to his liking.

When his departure from Red Bull was announced, the media were keen to pinpoint specific reasons for ending the almost-twenty-year relationship he'd enjoyed with the team, even though the turmoil all around him was plain to see. In the course of the year Red Bull would lose long-serving sporting director Jonathan Wheatley and Head of Strategy Will Courtenay, but Adrian was the model of discretion.

'I guess [I was considering it] over the winter a little bit, and then as events have unfolded this year I thought... I'm in a very lucky position where I don't need to work to live. I work because I enjoy it. I just felt that now was a good time to step back and take a bit of a break and take stock of life, and go travelling a bit.'

Something he would not say out loud was a perceived diminishing of his role in the success of the 2022/2023 seasons. Newey was known to be unhappy about others claiming credit for interpreting the new ground effect regulations so successfully. Christian Horner had a tendency to over-emphasise the role of the rest of the design group under technical director Pierre Wache. It was Newey who had the keys to the door. As he'd previously remarked, the 'porpoising' issue afflicted so many teams in 2022 but he knew how to minimise it. 'In that first test at Barcelona last year, it was very apparent that lots of people hadn't considered that at all.'

Weary of the same old story being peddled, he explained: 'There comes a point where I just felt, as Forrest Gump said: "I'm feeling a little bit tired."'

Williams, Ferrari, Alpine...?

With Adrian now available to work elsewhere, there was a clamour to know where that might be after he returned from his holiday in the Mediterranean. There were strong rumours that it would be Ferrari. Lewis Hamilton had said it would be a 'privilege' to work with Newey, and likewise Adrian expressed an interest in working with Lewis along with the sheer passion and history of the marque.

In the past he'd also expressed a desire to work with Fernando Alonso, who Red Bull were in serious discussions with after the 2013 Belgian Grand Prix (another potential blow to the RB driver programme). 'It's a regret that that never happened because I have a tremendous respect for Fernando,' he said. However, Fernando did buy his own super-spec version of the Newey-designed Aston Martin Valkyrie.

As his F1 suitors dwindled – McLaren and Mercedes counting themselves out of the race to sign him – it looked like a choice between Ferrari and Aston Martin. Fred Vasseur, boss of Ferrari, didn't want to get into a bidding war with Aston Martin, neither did he want to contemplate the restructuring of his engineering department to fit what Newey considered as best practice. Adrian might have been correct in his assessment of where the Scuderia were falling down, but the political fallout would have been colossal for Vasseur if he got it wrong.

Lawrence Stroll, father of Lance and owner of Aston Martin, had set about a major investment programme at the former Jordan team's Silverstone base, constructing a new, two-building campus, investing in a wind tunnel and hiring top personnel. He had hired former McLaren boss Martin Whitmarsh to oversee the development and coax an engine supply from Honda. He had also head-hunted former Mercedes engine boss Andy Cowell (the man responsible for the development of Mercedes' hybrid engines among others) as CEO. He had

NEWEY'S WINNERS

Adrian has been responsible for creating race-winning F1 cars for 15 drivers (figures in bold – stats up to the end of the 2024 season).

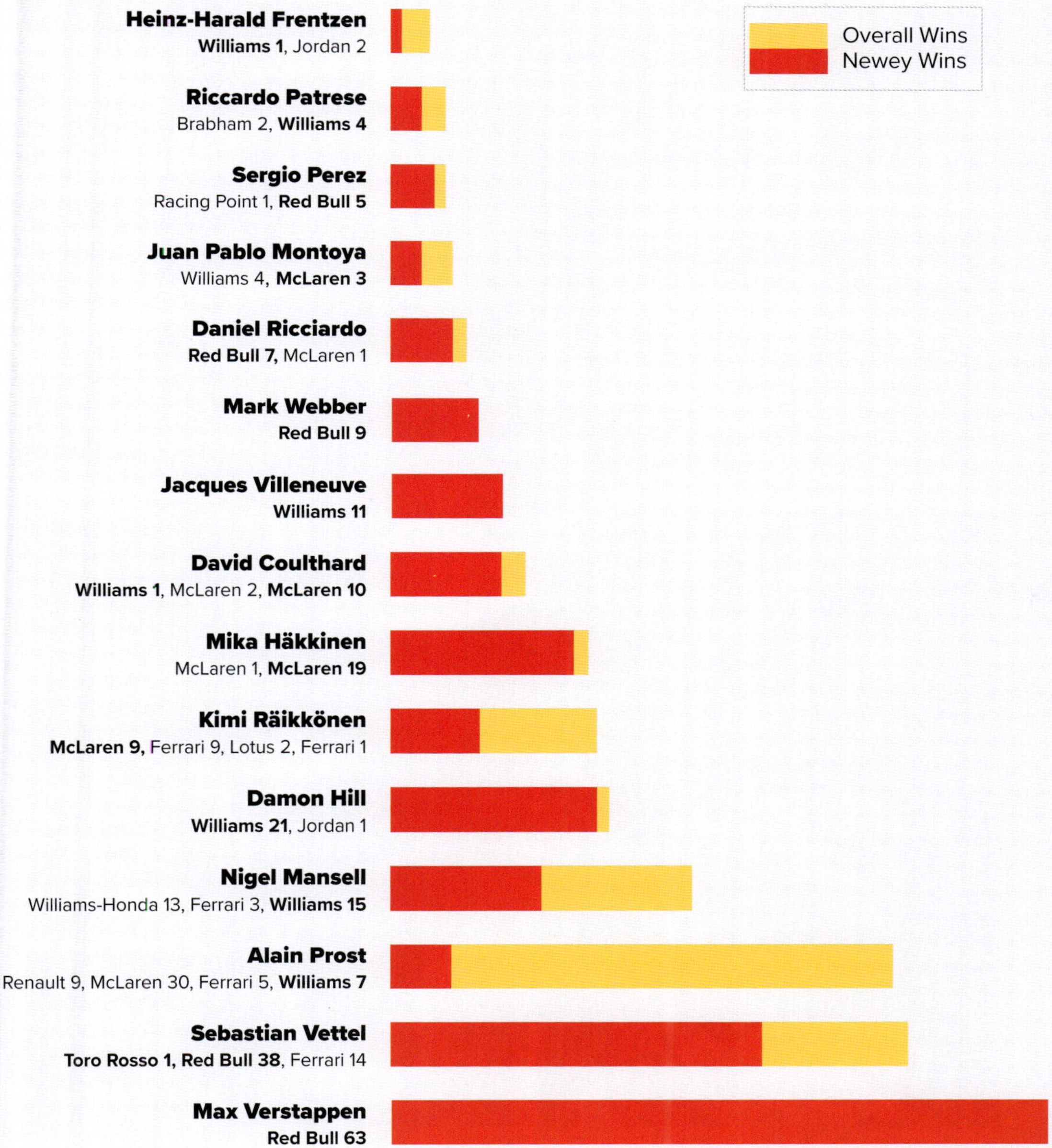

aramco
FORMULA ONE TEAM
sky
sports
MAADEN
cognizant
BOSS
JCB
SentinelOne

MAADEN
cognizant
BOSS
JCB
SentinelOne
aramco
FORMULA

LEFT: Adrian Newey's first appearance in Aston Martin team kit was at Monaco in 2025 where he put in quite a few interviews including with his old E-type Jag co-driver Martin Brundle.

BELOW: Prowling the grid at Monaco in 2025 and taking a good look at his former protege Rob Marshall's work at McLaren.

recruited former World Champions Sebastian Vettel and Fernando Alonso. Early in September, Stroll assembled his 800-odd staff in 'The Street' between two of the campus buildings and announced news of his new Managing Technical Partner. The roar of approval he got back was worthy of a Premier League crowd. They had been obliged to stay away during a 'secret' factory visit one Sunday morning in June when Newey had been given an advanced look at the facility.

Newey's official 'unveiling' at Aston Martin's HQ on 10 September was an unusual event, the first time anyone had arranged a press conference to announce the recruitment of an engineer. The team had beaten the likes of Williams, Alpine and Ferrari to the signature of a grand prix great, but he was still technically a Red Bull employee – he would not be free to work for Aston Martin until the end of March 2025. What's more, after the event he had to go back to Red Bull and work on the RB17 hypercar.

Wearing a powder-blue jacket Adrian strolled on stage to answer questions, having been introduced by Lawrence Stroll as, 'arguably the greatest in the world at what he does. He's a gentleman, he's a winner, he's a competitor, and he has the passion and desire to win, as do I and most of the people in this building.'

Asked immediately why Adrian chose Aston Martin, Lawrence Stroll was given as the answer. 'He's unique in that sense today,' said Newey, after listing the qualities of his relentless suitor. Newey preferred it old school, '... in that the team boss is the owner, like in the past with Frank Williams or Ron Dennis. The reality is, if you go back 20 years, then what we now call team principals were actually the owners of the teams.'

In the past, Newey had been keen to have a shareholding in the Williams team, but couldn't convince Frank otherwise. Eddie Jordan had been able to negotiate a share in the Aston Martin team for his 'talent', along with a salary reputed to rise to £30m a year with bonuses.

Adrian had also been impressed about the level of investment and infrastructure at Silverstone. The building blocks he needed to carefully put in place at Red Bull in 2005 were already there, including a wind tunnel. 'It's no easy thing to create on a greenfield site what Martin and Lawrence have created on this scale and to have a really nice warm creative feel to it.

'In any F1 team there are three principal technical departments. Aerodynamics, mechanical design and vehicle performance dynamics. It will initially be a case of trying to get good symmetry between those three departments and with Honda on the power unit side.'

LEFT: An ambition realised: Newey had previously worked with multiple World Champions – Prost, Senna, Vettel and Verstappen, but always regretted not having worked with either Lewis Hamilton or Fernando Alonso. Red Bull were in negotiations with the Spaniard just after the Belgian Grand Prix of 2013 but it all came to nothing.

Newey would be continuing his relationship with Honda engineers. The Japanese automotive giant had originally planned to quit F1 after the 2025 season, but the new engine rules that demanded a far greater electrical input had lured them back. Fernando Alonso was on hand for the press conference and offered his blue-chip endorsement. 'I would say he was an inspiration. I think thanks to Adrian and his talent and cars, we all got better as drivers, as engineers, as teams. We all had to raise the bar thanks to him, to be able to compete.

'I think[it's] an incredible day for the team. Lawrence's vision is taking shape with this building, with Adrian, with Honda, with Aramco, with a new wind tunnel ... Definitely the team of the future, I would say.'

Former McLaren and Aston Martin communications director Matt Bishop has known Adrian since the mid-1990s when he edited *F1 Racing* magazine. He believes Newey has possibly five working years left, the same time he needed to take Red Bull from pit lane jokers to multiple World Champions.

'His detractors say that he may not be as hungry as he once was. I disagree ... when you hire Newey, above all you are acquiring his thinking, and he needs time to think. He is not particularly adept at managing people, and he does not relish attending departmental meetings or answering admin-related emails, which is why he will be surrounded by other capable senior people who will do that kind of thing for him. What Newey loves, and is best at, is bending his remarkable mind to working out how to win in F1. I will never forget what Ron Dennis once said to me: "Adrian is the single most competitive person I've ever worked with." [Echoing Frank Williams] When you remind yourself that Ron worked with Ayrton Senna, I think you will agree that that is quite a claim.'

Chief trackside officer Mike Krack believes that the hiring of Newey will draw in talent. 'We are just more attractive as a team now – for partners, drivers, engineers. It's cool. When you are the fifth-best team you struggle to attract. We have a lot of young people who'd like to join us now, to work with Adrian.'

Focus on 2026

While the engine regulations had long been published, teams had only been allowed to enter their 2026 car designs in the wind tunnel from the beginning of 2025, following a sign-off of the technical regulations late in 2024. Thus Newey wouldn't be too far behind the curve when he started in March 2025. 'My concentration will clearly be on 2026,' he said, batting back suggestions that he might be employed on the 2025 car.

Andy Cowell had made sure everything was ready for Newey's arrival. 'From day one we made sure we prepared his working environment, he came in and went to meetings about the new rules, about the concepts we had worked on. We explained the countdown to the first test and the first race. And we pointed out all the deadlines for submitting information for the production of this 2026 car.

'He went straight to work with engineers to do sketches on his drawing board. He's in that design cycle to design fundamental parts of the car. Ninety per cent of the creation of a car is in the factory and that's where we want Adrian.

'He has his office, everyone who walks past says that whenever they see him he's always drawing on the whiteboard. He doesn't go to meetings, he doesn't answer emails, he's just putting together a fast car.'

In early August 2025 Aston Martin were able to confirm that Enrico Cardile had finally joined the team from Ferrari as chief technical officer. Cardile had left his post as Ferrari technical director in mid-2024 after agreeing to join Aston Martin, but the two teams had been engaged in a lengthy legal dispute over his start date. Cardile completed the trio of prestigious signings that Lawrence Stroll had brought to his own 'dream team'. First, ex-Mercedes engine guru Andy Cowell as CEO and team principal, Adrian Newey as managing technical partner and finally Enrico Cardile as chief technical officer to implement Newey's first Aston Martin F1 design.

The 2026 cars use sustainable fuels and feature power units that draw far more energy from the MGU-K unit. There is also an override system to give cars an extra overtaking (or defending) boost while following the car ahead, a similar feature to the DRS system.

Having seen Mercedes dominate in the past and having listened to the 2025 rumours that the engine factory at Brixworth was already ahead, Newey was circumspect about initial success with the 2026 car. 'There has to be a big chance that it's an engine formula at the start,' Newey told German magazine *Auto Motor und Sport*. 'I can't remember another time in Formula 1 when both the chassis regulations and the engine regulations have changed simultaneously, and where in this case the chassis regulations have been very much written to try to compensate, let's say, for the power unit regulations. So, it's an extra dimension.

'There has to be a chance that one manufacturer will come out well on top, and it will become a power-unit-dominated regulation, at least to start with. If it's on the electrical side, then there's much more ability to catch up if you're behind. And on the fuel side, which might play a role as well, there's flexibility in principle, but with dyno restrictions and the fact that everything's so optimised, you can't simply chuck a different fuel into an engine that hasn't been optimised for it.'

Adrian's first appearance in the green of Aston Martin came at the 2025 Monaco Grand Prix where he spent time in the garage talking to the race engineers and watching a reinvigorated Fernando Alonso take P7 in qualifying. Andy Cowell described it as 'embedding' himself in the team. Newey also answered questions about his programme. Despite the earlier assertion that he wouldn't be dealing with the 2025 car, given the team's wretched start to the 2025 season he had started having 'a few lunchtime chats' with the engineers.

In his Monaco interview he maintained, 'My first job has been, whilst designing and talking to everybody, to try and understand how the team works, its strengths and weaknesses, and set out a plan to try and boost the weaknesses,' he explained.

'There are a lot of very, very good people. We just need to try to get them working together perhaps in a slightly better organised way. That's simply a result of the roots of the team at Jordan, that became Force India, that became Racing Point. It was always a small but slightly overperforming team, to now, in a very short space of time, a very big team that in truth has been underperforming this year.'

ADRIAN NEWEY'S ENGLAND

One of the reasons that F1 is so successful in England is the concentration of teams in the 'motorsport valley', allowing personnel to swap around from team to team. Adrian's whole life has revolved around this small area.

Though Adrian was full of praise for the new wind tunnel he was far more circumspect about the driver-in-the-loop simulator. 'It needs a lot of work because it's not correlating at all at the moment, which is a fundamental research tool. Not having that is a limitation, but we've obviously got to work around it in the meantime. That's probably a two-year project, in truth. We're going to be a bit blind on that for some time. We've just got to try to use experience and best judgement.'

So, it would be shades of when he first joined other teams. He would have to

BELOW: Alonso at Monaco's Nouvelle Chicane in 2025. The team's sluggish start to the season put pressure on Newey to add his wisdom to the underperforming car.

rely on the biggest mental data bank in Formula 1.

'When I started, very little had been done on 2026 research, but we've done a huge amount since. It's a big challenge, and I think deadlines are coming up very quickly,' he said. 'Lead times have got much longer because cars are more complicated and they take longer to design and manufacture, and the research tools are much more sophisticated. My main focus at the moment is working with everybody on what I call the fundamentals of the car, which are the bits of the car that you can't change during a season, so front and rear suspension layout, length of the fuel tank, all that sort of thing. If we can get those right, then the bodywork and wings, etc., you can try to develop through the year.'

Newey confessed that his 3 March start date was later than he would have liked. 'The rules came out in their final form on the first of January. I'm sure there was enough known about the regulations that a decent body of work could have been done, and no doubt was done by many teams prior to that,' he explained. 'So, starting later than that, you're always chasing and playing catch-up, but it is what it is.'

Playing catch-up has meant one of his most intensive periods of work since the early days of Red Bull. 'I had the weekend off two weeks ago, but other than that, it's been pretty much full on since I started in March. My wife says I go into a design trance. When I get into this period of intense concentration and I tend to not see left and right, all my processing power is going into one area, which is trying to design a fast racing car ...'

Speaking to Motorsport Network boss James Allen, Andy Cowell admitted that Adrian's comments at Monaco, especially about the simulator taking two years to get up to speed, had spurred the team on.

'The great thing with Adrian is he knows the level that we need to get to. So he's setting high standards,' said the former Mercedes AMG High Performance Powertrains (HPP) boss. 'I'm setting tough standards within the organisation. And then it's about how quickly can we get there. Is it going to take us two years to get there? No, it's not. Is Adrian provoking people? Yes, he is. We are all setting high standards to achieve. And the competitive advantage comes from how quickly you achieve it.

'Everybody in the factory that I've spoken to that's working around the design team is going, "Well, we'll show him! We'll turn it into months rather than years."

'Adrian is focused on the design of the race car, the architecture, and the detailed considerations. He's been in the industry a long time, as have I, and we know our strengths and our weaknesses. I think a strength that we've both got is that we can just talk openly to each other.'

One of the motivating factors in Newey's move was the chance to work with Fernando Alonso. His long-held wish to develop a car with either Fernando or Lewis Hamilton had finally come true.

'Fernando, he's such a cool character,' Newey said. 'I've said before that you can only work with so many drivers, but two drivers I always wanted, that I felt I would enjoy working with, were Lewis and Fernando, and I couldn't work with both, so at least I got one of them. It's only when you get to the racetrack that you really start to develop that relationship, so I'm looking forward to that developing a little bit this season, but particularly next season.'

His first trackside appearance of 2025 in Monte Carlo was a joy for Alonso, who, frankly, was going backwards in the 2024 season. 'It was fantastic,' the

BELOW: Adrian and Fernando chat in the paddock in Mexico before the 2022 Mexican GP. Little did Fernando Alonso know that three years after he was driving for the Alpine team he and Adrian would both be at Aston Martin.

BELOW: The FIA render of the design template for the 2026 car, first released in 2024. Intriguingly, Newey has pointed out that the new regulations allow for 'more flexibility for innovation and different approaches than first meets the eye ...'

two-time World Champion said of working with Newey. 'I think the way he sees things on the car, even statically [in] the pit lane or on the grid, also in the garage spotting some things that we could have done better or do better in the future.

'His presence in the meeting room is always special – not intimidating, but I think the level of the team was higher thanks to his presence because everyone was more focused, more into the details of the car. People who were talking in the meeting, they know that they cannot say anything too far from the truth because he will spot it, so I think that was great to witness and I hope next year, with more races that he will come [to], we'll keep learning from him and getting better as a team.'

9

ASTON MARTIN
009
HEART OF RACING
HYPER CAR
MICHELIN
ROLEX

THE SPORTS CARS

PREVIOUS PAGE: The Aston Martin Valkyrie in its 2025 WEC specification.

LEFT: Unlike many sports car collectors, Adrian Newey likes to take his to track events. One of his Le Mans cars is the V12 Ferrari 512M from 1969 which he raced up the hill at Goodwood.

Ever since Adrian Newey tired of his 1:12 scale Tamiya kits, he has been designing sports cars. His first major project was a sports car with ground effect, destined to be his final-year coursework at Southampton University. At March Engineering he adapted an existing chassis into the series-winning March 83G, followed by the 84G. From then his career took him into open-wheel racing, but he never lost the childhood appreciation of classic sports cars, and his love of driving the fastest road-going machinery has meshed with designing two of the greatest 'track day' cars.

The driving side started off with classic car rallies in his 1938 Jaguar SS100. Mostly they were regularity runs, driving each segment of a stage in a specified time at a specified average speed. Occasionally there were sections away from public roads where the speed limit need not be observed and the ever-competitive Adrian enjoyed these the most. One of his earliest sports cars – in the Newey Collection – was the Ford GT40, which broke Ferrari's stranglehold on race wins in the classic Ford vs Ferrari battle of the 1960s.

Le Mans

'It's an iconic car, a very pretty car, and one of the last cars from that era that you could also drive on the road,' he recounted to the Le Mans racing website. 'You could race it, then jump back in and drive it home if you wished to. I think the other classic Le Mans cars for me are the Ferrari P4 – the same era and very pretty car – and then the Porsche 917 and Ferrari 512. We're talking mid- to late-60s, very early 70s, when I was devouring *Autosport* as a teenager.'

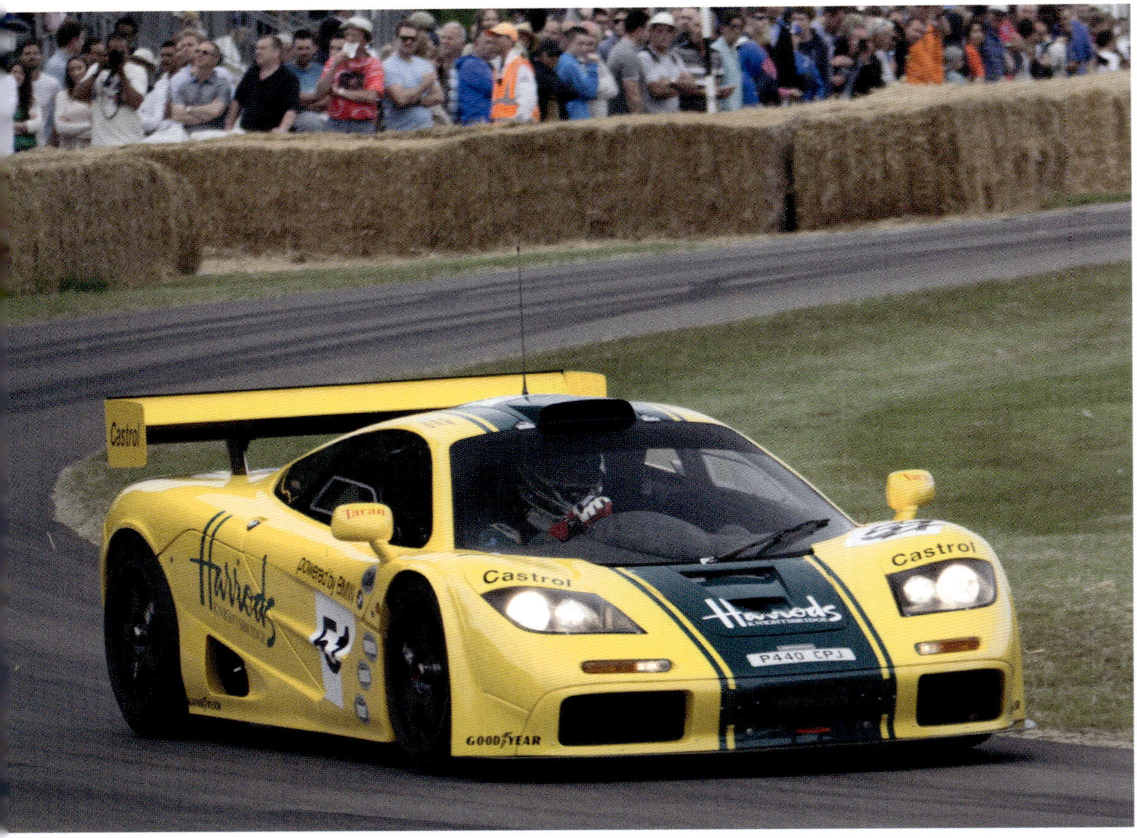

Adrian managed to import an original GT40 from the States, which he competed with in a number of historic races before taking it to the Le Mans Classic in July 2006. Running in second place he was following established racer Ray Bellm down the Mulsanne Straight when he suffered brake failure approaching the second chicane. The GT40 skidded along the guard rails before thumping into the barrier that divides the chicanes, wrecking the car. Photos taken at the time show a mangled wreck and Adrian, who walked away mercifully unscathed, surveying the wreck, head in hands. It would be rebuilt, but it was a salutary lesson in the strength needed for sports cars and the solidity of the GT40.

His love of sports cars remained undimmed. He was soon competing again, this time driving a Jaguar E-type lightweight in September's Goodwood Revival meeting. He was lapping traffic during practice when he was involved in an accident at the kink on the Lavant Straight. After spinning across the grass,

ABOVE: The Ferrari F430 GT2 run by top team AF Corse at the 2007 24 Heures du Mans. Newey's stint in the wet was one of the most frightening driving experiences of his life.

LEFT: Newey is also the owner of a McLaren F1 sports car, similar to this example running at Goodwood. Adrian bought a short-tailed GTR as raced at Le Mans.

Newey's car hit the barriers with the right rear corner taking the impact.

'The damage to the car is quite light but I must have hit my head on the rollbar, which knocked me unconscious,' Adrian reported. 'I came round in the ambulance feeling a bit dazed.'

He was taken to St. Richards' Hospital in Chichester for precautionary checks. IndyCar racer, Scotsman Dario Franchitti was also taken to hospital and detained overnight after suffering a big crash in a similar Jaguar E-type lightweight. He was placed in a bed right next to Adrian. 'Apparently Dario and I shared several 'goldfish' moments during recuperation in the hospital. We were both turning to each other every 20 minutes asking the same question, "what are you doing here?"'

Newey would return regularly to the Goodwood events, and in 2007 revisited Le Mans. This time he would be at the back of the professional field as opposed to at the front of the historic 'gentleman racers'.

Adrian had obtained his racing licence after tuition with experienced driver-coach Joe Macari who had become a family friend. 'It really started as a pub chat,' Newey recalled in an interview with the official 24 Heures du Mans website. 'Joe said, "Look, why don't we have a go at Le Mans?" So, the three of us, me, Joe and Ben Aucott, who was the owner of a Ferrari F430 GT2 car said, "Okay, let's do this."

'Joe had a few contacts, of course, and managed to pull some strings. And so we got the entry [with AF Corse] for the 2007 race. And I think at that point I had done the grand total of about 12 races, something like that.' Adrian managed to get a dispensation from Christian Horner to skip the Canadian Grand Prix which would have interfered with preparations.

18

GIVES YOU
sparco

START
START

LEFT: Two photos from 2006 as Adrian Newey waits on the grid in his beloved Ford GT40. He was taking part in a support race for historic sports cars before the 2006 British Grand Prix at Silverstone.

BELOW LEFT: The vintage Ferrari 512M roars away from the line at the Goodwood Festival of Speed.

BOTTOM RIGHT: The Lightweight E-Type competing at Goodwood.

'And it was off to Le Mans, which is very much in at the deep end. This was in the days before Pro-Am. We were, I believe, the only all-amateur driver line-up on the starting grid at Le Mans, up against the pros. All we wanted to do was enjoy ourselves. Keep out of trouble. Make sure we didn't get in anybody's way and try and get to the finish. That was the target.

'There was a lot of rain during the race quite early on and then very heavy in the early hours of Sunday morning. I did a triple stint in that wet, wet part which was pretty "eyes wide open" the whole way through.

'I do remember my race engineer coming on the radio and saying, "Adrian, the Panoz is behind you. It's catching you at two seconds a lap," and I came back and said, "I bet he hasn't got a wife and four children" because I was absolutely petrified in the car but managed to keep it on the island.' They finished in 22nd place overall, completing 308 laps and were still ahead of the Panoz at the finish.

The experience of driving at Le Mans and sharing a winning car with Martin Brundle at Goodwood has helped him understand the pressure that falls upon race drivers to perform. And when successive Red Bull protégés have climbed into the challenging second seat alongside Max Verstappen, Adrian has struck a sympathetic figure.

Valkyrie

Having banked his experience of the Le Mans 24 Hours race, when the new hybrid engine era arrived in Formula 1 in 2014, with no prospect of a competitive engine from Renault, he had again flirted with a job offer from Maranello. Which means the concept that became the Aston Martin Valkyrie could even have ended up as a Ferrari.

Christian Horner revealed to American podcaster Dax Shepard how close Adrian was to joining the Scuderia in 2014. According to Horner, Ferrari made Newey a very attractive offer to design their F1 car for 2015, reuniting with Sebastian Vettel: 'Ferrari came hard for him,' Horner revealed. 'They promised him the world. You can have a Hollywood lifestyle, flying to the factory from Monaco every day. Not pay any tax. You can design a road car.'

Newey had previously owned a Ferrari 288 GTO and would go on to own a 1960s Ferrari 275GTB, so the offer of a Newey-signature Ferrari was very tempting. 'Adrian came very close to leaving,' Horner said. 'He was within about half an hour of signing.'

The Red Bull boss countered by offering to let Newey work on other projects that interested him, including the creation of a hypercar. At the time, Aston Martin was the title sponsor of the F1 team, so Horner arranged a hasty meeting with then-CEO, Andy Palmer, and pitched him the idea. 'Look, we've got arguably the best designer of all time. You've got a great brand. We're not going to finance the car, but it would make sense to bring these two things together, and that was a deal literally made in a pub in England.'

BELOW: The launch of the Aston Martin Valkyrie at Silverstone in 2019. Aston test driver Chris Goodwin (far right) was tasked with exploratory laps in 'Verification Prototype 1'.

Adrian stayed – continuing to design the Red Bull F1 car but diverting half of his time to Red Bull Advanced Technologies' projects. And while one was working with an America's Cup yachting team, the other was the design of the Valkyrie.

Apart from owning a classic Ford GT40, Adrian owns another Le Mans winner, the Gordon Murray-designed McLaren F1. 'When I first joined McLaren from Williams, in 1997, the [road car] F1 programme was still going. I was impressed with it as a car and I also drove one briefly.'

At the time, despite his mega salary, he couldn't afford to buy one. By the time he got to Red Bull, he could. And it shaped his future thinking on the Valkyrie. 'I was more interested in one of the ex-race cars, what's called a short-tailed GTR, which is the type of car that won at Le Mans. To me, the race cars drive slightly better than the road cars do, in as much as the road car's set-up is quite soft and can be little bit wayward.'

The McLaren F1 was a product of the early 1990s, and vehicle technology had come a long way in 25 years. Newey's idea was to design a Le Mans Prototype (LMP1) racer which could also be driven on the road.

'We didn't do any benchmarking against potential competitor cars because we wanted to try and establish a new genre of car that was more track-biased than other road cars have been, while still making it usable on the road,' he told *Autoweek*. 'The analogy I always had in my mind was a modern superbike: incredible performance but you can take it to the shops. And you need to really have your wits about you or it will bite you. When you really enjoy it is when you get to take it on track.

In comments made to BBC's TopGear.com, he said, 'I always design a car as a package, and then details fall out of that evolution of the package, the overall layout, I feel, has worked quite well – trying to marry performance against aesthetics, against the emotion of driving a car.'

Lurking in the rear of the Valkyrie/AM-RB 001 is a growling 6.5-litre V12 Cosworth engine pumping out 1,000bhp, allied to an e-boost that adds an additional 160bhp.

When it comes to the rev counter, it hits the red line at 11,100rpm not surprisingly producing a high degree of cabin noise in the carbon-fibre passenger compartment. For driveability it has an e-motor for reverse and low-speed manoeuvring, making it far less cumbersome and easier to handle in tight spaces, problems exacerbated by the driver's low position.

'With hindsight, we underestimated the amount of electronic boxes, safety equipment and general paraphernalia that's now associated with modern road cars. Some of that is to do with emissions, some of it with safety regulations. That has certainly made the car a little bit heavier than we initially hoped and expected,' he admitted.

'It's a car that has stretched or pushed the performance boundary, particularly the

BELOW: The Valkyrie on display at the Geneva Motor Show.

RIGHT: In advance of its 2025 Le Mans 24 Hours debut, Aston Martin put on display the ten WEC-spec Valkyries that were up for sale.

007
007
PIRELLI
P ZERO

007
007
001
001
002
003

track performance boundary, of a car that's hopefully reasonably comfortable, and civilised to drive on the road, to a much higher level than any other car has done.'

Lawrence Stroll started investing in the Aston Martin company from 2020 – and the change of ownership meant that cars were not fully released to the paying public until after Red Bull had ceased their involvement. The original plan was for customer deliveries to begin in 2018.

'Red Bull Advanced Technologies was set up for exactly this project, but it's grown and matured and we've got quite a lot of commercial projects on the books now,' Newey said on the Valkyrie's debut appearance at the Goodwood Festival of Speed. 'That makes it easier to take on a road car [project] or a track-biased car that can be put on the road in a shorter timescale because of the extra experience we've gained.'

LEFT: The Valkyrie belonging to Newey's driver coach and Le Mans co-driver, Joe Macari of Joe Macari Performance Cars.

BELOW: The front wing and front suspension of the RB17.

'So yes, absolutely, we would like to do another vehicle. Exactly what that is, who it's targeted at, is subject to debate. Watch this space is probably the easiest way to put it...'

RB17 Hypercar

That 'space' would be filled by the RB17. While the Valkyrie was built with Le Mans in mind, the RB17 would be even faster than a World Endurance Championship-spec car. 'The idea I started to formulate really was, "OK, is it possible to create a two-seater track car that is capable of Formula 1 lap times but accessible to all drivers so that they can enjoy that performance potential and grow with the car and learn about it?"' Newey told the Goodwood Festival of Speed website.

His original drawings of the car were made over the Christmas break of 2020/21, when his workload could not have been greater. He had the 2021 RB16B to fine-tune and develop over the course of a championship-winning season, and he needed to begin research on what would become the RB18 to an entirely new set of regulations for 2022.

'The first car I drew was actually four-wheel drive in as much as it had the electric motor on the front axle. Having done a load of simulation, it turned out because we're not working to a weight limit, that it's actually faster to save the

weight and put the electric motor in the rear axle and make it two-wheel drive, which I was very happy about.'

As can be expected with a track-day car designed to be driven to the track, the humdrum additions of everyday driving necessities impinged on the concept. Adrian's experience of driving its predecessor, the Valkyrie, at the Goodwood Festival of Speed hillclimb had made him fully acquainted with the road-manoeuvring qualities needed for a hypercar – not so much the blast up past

Goodwood House, more the trundling into position backwards and forwards.

'It's quite a lot of manoeuvring simply to get onto the track in the first place,' he revealed. 'You have to do a lot of low-speed running when you're coming back down the hill and queuing up to get up it. It accidentally combines all the features that you might have in "normal" day use – driving slowly in traffic, then driving briskly on an open bit of road.'

BELOW: The RB17 on display at the Goodwood Festival of Speed in 2024, photographed by seasoned F1 snapper Mark Thompson.

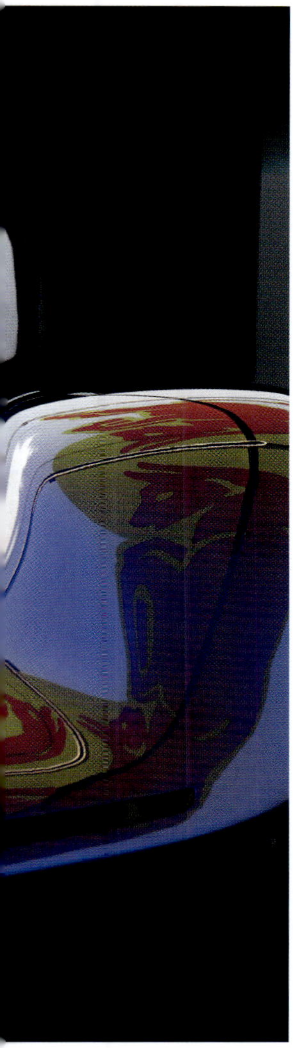

Like the Valkyrie, the RB17 was designed with different levels of complexity, but with the basic premise that anyone could get in the car and drive it in its simplest set-up. Three years of development went into the car from 2021 to January 2024.

'When we first started, to achieve the performance level we wanted it was going to be a twin-turbo V8, because that's the engine that gave the power we wanted to achieve from the combustion side of it.'

Except Adrian didn't like the 'aural experience' of a V8. When F1 moved into the hybrid era he hated the lack of noise. So he asked the team: 'Can we do a normally aspirated engine that's capable of 1,000 horsepower that still comes in under 150kg? The answer, of course, is yes if you rev it, and by going to pneumatic valves we achieved that.'

So the car went from a V8 twin-turbo to a V10, 4.5-litre, normally aspirated engine revving to 15,000rpm, producing more than 1,000 horsepower. If that's not quite enough there is an extra e-boost that adds an additional 160bhp.

What beginners notice most about race cars is the stiffness of the suspensions. If the car is designed to emulate F1 lap times then it also needs to be wound up tight. 'Active suspension is probably the biggest single key in that,' Newey explained. 'Because that means that the software can change the balance of the car very easily. It obviously has to be mapped for that, while the active aerodynamics on top allow you to change the downforce level quite a lot. These will all be adjustable from inside the car, to adapt the RB17's response through corner entry, apex, or exit.'

The RB17 will be infinitely adjustable, but with basic settings so that, as Newey says, 'You're not completely intimidated and overwhelmed by it, but with practice and application you can get the enjoyment of driving it, but also get the enjoyment of the challenge of bettering your lap time.'

Christian Horner described the RB17 as 'Adrian off the leash'. While many supercars can reach 350kph, at under 900kg the RB17 gets there a lot quicker and brakes impressively. Many passengers in the 1998 McLaren MP4/98T, two-seater, designed to give team partners and sponsors an experience of F1 speed, reported

LEFT AND BELOW: The RB17 on display at Red Bull HQ. The numbering of the car was made possible by the F1 team skipping straight from the RB16Bin 2021 to the RB18 in 2022. The RB17 is expected to emulate F1 performance.

that it wasn't necessarily the acceleration that made them gasp, it was the incredibly short braking distances.

The limited run of 50 cars was launched in July 2024 at the Goodwood Festival of Speed. In Red Bull's official press release Horner announced, 'Combining technical innovation, achievement and emotional appeal, the RB17 is a landmark car. I'm very proud of the team and am delighted to see it make its world debut. We expect the RB17 to be a future classic.'

Alongside the Aston Martin Valkyrie, which made its debut at Le Mans in 2025, that is a given.

10

14
Red

DESIGN PHILOSOPHIES

If it were possible to quantify the amount of thought Adrian Newey has put into motorsport technology over more than four decades of design, it would be an impressive figure. Ideas strike him everywhere – on flights, on the beach, in showers and, most worrying of all, while driving in his car. In his autobiography he confessed, 'Many were the times I'd arrive late, having taken a wrong turn, or missed my junction, deep in thought. So now, for reasons of effective time management and a desire for punctuality, I have a driver.'

One thing that is universally known about Adrian is that he is still stuck in the 1980s. Newey is no different from contemporaries John Barnard, Patrick Head and Ross Brawn in that they worked with a drawing board. Except Adrian's career has gone on the longest.

'If I were to convert to CAD (Computer Aided Design) I'd have to learn something new and not only is there a time penalty to doing that, but there's the question of whether I'd be as fluent in my new language as I was in my old,' he told the High Performance podcast. 'I keep at least two people occupied taking my paper drawings and turning them into CAD drawings. And these are just the ones I think are worth transcribing. It's usually taken several iterations to get to that point: my consumption of erasers is only just behind my consumption of pencil lead.

'I grew up on the drawing board. It's my first language. If I was a younger generation, I wouldn't, I'd be on CAD. And I don't think there's an underlying advantage or disadvantage to one or the other. And I think actually now the CAD is a stronger tool.

'If I go back even ten years, the guys on the CAD would take such a long time constructing their drawing that they would be reluctant to change it, whereas I'm more than happy to get the rubber out, and probably the lines I end up with, probably 50 per cent of them at least have been rubbed out at some point, because I keep changing until I'm happy with it.

'Whereas now, with what's called parametrics, these guys can put a few dots and crosses down, create their history file, and then they can change it quite quickly and easily. So I'm starting to feel slightly disadvantaged on the drawing board.'

The other disadvantage is that he is only drawing in two dimensions. 'I seem to

BELOW: Two of Adrian Newey's great inspirations, driver Graham Hill and designer Colin Chapman. The adolescent car fanatic could never have dreamed that he would not only own a race-ready Lotus, but race engineer the two-time World Champion's son.

have quite a good ability to visualise something in 3D and then put it down onto paper in 2D, whereas the CAD system does free you of that. You don't have to go through the 2D to do that. You can start straight in 3D.'

Although the wind tunnel is Newey's reassuring 'fix' on the progress of his designs, he has embraced the speed at which computational fluid dynamics (CFD), has speeded up the design process, enabling him to see what works and what does not. 'It's an amazing tool that really didn't reach maturity in Formula 1 until the late 90s. I'll look at the CFD and I'll sketch from that some ideas and then draw something.

'My influences included, first and foremost, Colin Chapman, obviously because he was a significant designer, but also because Dad had three Lotus Elans, including a Plus 2, two of them built from kits. Then as I got a bit older I

became fascinated by the Chaparrals and Jim Hall. It's interesting how often things that are now commonplace in F1 were first popularised in sports car racing: monocoques and disc brakes for the Jaguar D-type; wings with the Chaparrals, plus the fan car concept; fuel injection too. Even today racing teams are not big enough to be research institutes, so we plagiarise and use whatever we see available. That's something that hasn't changed.'

Something that Adrian borrowed from aviation was the airbox above a driver's head. Back at Williams in 1996 he'd been struggling with the airflow off the top of Damon's helmet, which was not going into the airbox hence losing engine performance.

ABOVE: Jim Hall's Chaparral 2A (No.66), which evolved all the way through to the 2H of 1968 (No.7 car in the background). The 2C was the first Chaparral to use an in-car adjustable rear wing.

'In August, on our summer holiday, I took an internal flight from Barbados to one of the little islands. I looked out the window, it was a little turboprop, and I looked at the engine intake, which was just below the propeller, but the shape above that engine intake was such they had obviously come up with a similar problem relative to the propeller. They had shaped the engine intake appropriately. So that's what we then put on to the following 1997 car at Williams. And now it's the standard.

'I'm often asked whether flair and innovation are constricted in the modern age,' he told *Motor Sport* magazine. 'My answer is it's different today. The big visual changes – chassis and bodywork shape, engine configuration and the number of cylinders – yes, it's true: the cars nowadays look relatively similar to each other and that's a product of regulation and convergence. But there is still a lot of concept work that goes into these cars, it's just in a more confined area. As the rules become more restrictive you get hemmed into smaller areas, but equally the tools keep developing to allow you to explore those areas in more detail. So I don't think that makes it less interesting, just different. It's a bit like comparing a Spitfire to a modern fighter jet.

'Having said that, I would love the rules to be more open. There are two arguments given for having restrictive rules. One is to try to control costs, and the other which has never really been advertised but is definitely a factor, is the fear that one team would read a more open rulebook better than others and disappear into the distance.'

In 2010 Newey created the Red Bull X1 (also known as the X2010) for video game Gran Turismo 5 and 6. It was an exercise in what could be designed if there were no rules in place hemming designers in. It was a virtual creation, not a real road car, but it served as a blueprint for pushing the boundaries of motorsport design. The X1 was designed in collaboration with Kazunori Yamauchi, the creator of the Gran Turismo series. The X1's concept was based on a low-air-resistance, single-seat, covered-wheel prototype. The goal was to create the fastest possible racing car, free from regulations, making it potentially superior to a real Formula 1 car.

'With the cost cap now in place taking care of the first part, there's a good argument to open the rules up and get some more visual differentiation. But even with the very restrictive regulations, that can still happen!' As was abundantly clear in 2023. 'Also bear in mind that since the cost cap has been introduced the competitive order hasn't really changed that much.'

Despite Red Bull having overshot the very first cost cap in 2021, Newey believes it is by and large a positive move. 'I do think trying to contain an arms race is a good thing to do. But I'm not convinced the way it's done is right. The cost cap has a lot of shortfalls, some of them not immediately obvious when it was introduced. For instance, because it is a cost cap and not a people cap we as an industry can't keep up with inflation. So F1 has gone from being the best-paid engineering industry in the world to most definitely not any more. A lot of start-up electric car companies, tech companies and other racing series are now actually better paid as an industry than F1. At Red Bull we weren't alone in losing people

LEFT AND BELOW: In 2010 the unleashed Adrian Newey was given free rein to create a car not governed by rules and regulations. The result was the Red Bull X1 introduced in the video games Gran Turismo 5 and 6.

– not to other teams, but other industries. The same is true when it comes to hiring undergraduates. We are no longer offering the highest salaries.

'The car changed again in 2022. I think it's a shame they have become so big and heavy,' he said, though acknowledging that it's a necessity if F1 is to incorporate 50 per cent electric power and all its attendant batteries. 'In our twentieth year celebrations we had RB1 alongside RB20 – and RB1 now looks like a Formula 3 car. It seemed quite big at the time. F1 has always had a habit of popularising things in road cars. Now road cars are getting ever bigger and heavier as well, and in the drive to be green it's the absolute opposite of what we should be doing. People can argue about where the energy should come from

– battery, petrol or hydrogen – but the thing that is going to make it most green is using less energy and of course the bigger and heavier the car the more energy it's going to use. Pretty simple stuff.

'Personally I feel we need to be looking at making much smaller, lighter, aerodynamically efficient cars. Maybe if we did that it would help popularise a desire in the road-car market to look at smaller, lighter cars too.

ABOVE: Adrian supervises a paddock full of his creations at the twentieth anniversary of the Red Bull marque at Goodwood.

ABOVE RIGHT: Like FIA chief Mohammed Ben Sulayem and Max Verstappen, Newey is a big fan of the screaming output from a conventional V10.

'We're facing another generational change in 2026. We know the rough principles of what the FIA is trying to achieve, which was initially a desire for a 50-50 combustion-engine/electric mix. Whether that's a good direction or not, it's probably best I don't comment. There is a drive to make the cars a bit lighter but the reality is it's a heavy power unit, so there is only so far you can go.

'If governments insist on zero emissions from tailpipes that doesn't leave the internal combustion engine in a good place. But if you go for net zero that opens up all sorts of other possibilities. Biofuels and e-fuels are an interesting and growing concept.'

Newey would have been intrigued by the proposal FIA president Mohammed Ben Sulayem put forward in 2025 about re-introducing V10 engines with net zero emissions. Having only just lured Audi, Ford, Cadillac and Honda back onto the grid with the concept of 50-50 propulsion it seemed a bizarrely mistimed move – but one that appealed to those like Adrian who love the visceral roar of the V10 (as one might expect from a man with a collection of high-powered former racing cars.

The new engines, apart from being quieter and heavier were envisaged to be slower than their 2025 counterparts. Thus to gain some of that speed back, the FIA has allowed designers to use something that for decades has been off limits – movable aerodynamic devices.

From 2026, all-new active aerodynamics systems, involving movable front and rear wings, have been introduced. This will allow for greater cornering speeds and lower drag on straights to regain the loss of engine power. As the most experienced aerodynamicist in F1, this can only play to Adrian Newey's strengths.

The BBC's Andrew Benson asked Adrian if he had any regrets over a career in which he has re-written Formula 1's record books. The graphic at right shows the titles he has won in comparison to his peers.

His initial thoughts were of Senna: 'Well, clearly first and foremost to have had a longer relationship with Ayrton,' Newey immediately replied.

'The truth is, first of all, I try to live in the present and the future and not the past. Regrets? No. I just feel tremendously lucky to have had the opportunities I've had and to have worked with the people I have done and met the people I have done.'

ABOVE: Newey has designed cars for two out of three of the greatest drivers of the twenty-first century and counts himself lucky. This is the stellar podium from the Canadian Grand Prix of 2023.

TITLE WINNERS

An introductory profile to Adrian Newey is often accompanied by the tally of World Championship titles he has won. In isolation it is difficult to evaluate, so to put it into perspective we have compiled a grid of F1's top designers and team principals, combining their constructors' (since 1958) and drivers' (since 1950) titles. Adrian Newey's total is made of 12 constructors' titles (5 Williams, 1 McLaren and 6 Red Bull) and 14 drivers' titles (Mansell, Prost, Hill, Villeneuve, Häkkinen (2), Vettel and Verstappen (4 each) – which puts him on pole.

ADRIAN NEWEY
Williams, McLaren, Red Bull
26

ENZO FERRARI
Ferrari
17

PATRICK HEAD
Williams
16

ROSS BRAWN
Benetton, Ferrari, Brawn
16

TOTO WOLFF
Mercedes
15

COLIN CHAPMAN
Vanwall, Lotus
14

RON DENNIS
McLaren
14

CHRISTIAN HORNER
Red Bull
14

RORY BYRNE
Benetton, Ferrari
12

MAURO FORGHIERI
Ferrari
11

GORDON MURRAY
Brabham, McLaren
10

FLAVIO BRIATORE
Benetton, Renault
7

JOHN COOPER
Cooper
4

ADRIAN NEWEY BY HIS PEERS

Adrian commands a tremendous amount of respect, not only from the drivers he's worked with, but from his rivals down the pit lane.

ALAIN PROST

(Williams)

" I loved talking to Adrian. Adrian is listening to you, asking questions all the time. You never have an argument with Adrian. You're talking with Adrian and he is listening, and then he does what he thinks is the best, but he never tells you what he's going to do – or if you're right or you're wrong. Nothing. Just listening and talking.

I love that, you know, that is why he's the best. But also the ways he is working and listening, and it's fantastic for the engineers working with him, it brings energy and synergy in terms of the brain, that capacity is fantastic. "

DAVID COULTHARD

(Williams, McLaren and Red Bull)

" What distinguishes Adrian from the others is that he thinks like a racing driver. He is a hobby racer himself. He will not frighten Max [Verstappen] with his lap times, but I think he participated in the historic Grand Prix of Monte Carlo with his Lotus 49. He is ready to try himself out, and that's why he understands what a driver is talking about when he talks about understeer on the track or understeer when switching to oversteering at the corner exit. He knows exactly what that means because he has experienced it himself. I think that really helps him.'

He's a complete package. Today there are specialists, people who are materials engineers. They know which materials are the right ones to make parts of the car. This is their area of expertise, they are not racing drivers per se. They are not engineers, they are not performance engineers. They are materials engineers. You need a lot of people who specialise in a certain role, but Adrian's leadership skills are based on the fact that he really understands the process from concept to design to delivery and driving.

I think this certainly gives him a competitive advantage over much more highly qualified engineers ... You need people in practice who are creative and perform. "

MARTIN BRUNDLE
(Goodwood co-driver and Sky commentator)

“I'm sure this is his last roll of the dice with a big team, and he'll want it to be a success. You can be sure that, for big-picture stuff, he's the man you want looking at it. Aston Martin, like other teams, have a long way north of a thousand people and you need to keep them incentivised. They don't want to be bit-part players.

It's a delicate operation to introduce Adrian into a team like that. But he's worked with Honda while at Red Bull so will be helpful on that front. He'll have something in his head already about the really massive change of aerodynamics that go with the new power units of 2026. I'd be sure that, for big-picture stuff, he'll have critical ideas.

Also, he's ruthless. If Adrian wants something, he'll get it. Even if it seems impossible time-wise or budget-wise, he will persist until he gets what he knows is right. That's why you need a team of some might to make the best use of him.”

FERNANDO ALONSO
(Aston Martin)

“I would say Adrian was more an inspiration thanks to his talent and cars. We all got better as a driver, as engineers; we all had to raise the bar thanks to him, to be able to compete.”

SIR JACKIE STEWART
(Founder: Race Against Dementia)

“We have had many great drivers in Formula 1, but few who can impact a team as much as Adrian Newey. He is a man with a unique perspective on F1 cars and understands more than most of us can dream of understanding.”

DANIEL RICCIARDO
(Red Bull)

" My dad, when I signed with Red Bull, was like, 'Oh, you're gonna get to work with Adrian.' That was exciting for him as well.

Walking into his office is kind of intimidating because of the big design board, he's probably going to ask me things I have no idea what he's talking about. I was thinking, 'Don't ask me too many questions, let's just keep this fairly basic for my own good,' but also he's a fan of motorsport – he gets involved, whether it's Goodwood, the Revival or things like this. He's just a fan deep down like all of us. "

ABOVE: The 'Best of' line-up of past and present Red Bull drivers at the 20th Anniversary celebrations at Goodwood House.

DAMON HILL
(Williams)

" I really respect Adrian, he is a really good driver-engineer who listens to the driver. You could tell he wanted to hear what you had to say, which is really encouraging. He was very good at making me a part of the team. He is very competitive and also has a sense of humour ... but he doesn't like to lose. "

ANDREW BENSON
(BBC F1 Correspondent)

" Newey is as close to a guarantee of success as it gets in F1. On one level, his skill is to see in an arcane and complex set of technical regulations the secrets of what is possible to unlock the most performance. And performance in F1 is primarily to do with aerodynamics.

How can he do that better than probably anyone in history? It's to do with the way his brain processes the nuances of airflow. Newey is an aerodynamicist by trade, but he doesn't just apply the physics and look at the numbers produced in wind tunnels and computer simulations. He can imagine the air and how it will move around the car, how the various flows will interact with each other. "

CHRISTIAN HORNER

(Red Bull)

"He's a unique character. He has tremendous creativity. And a huge eye for detail. But he's also very practical. He's come from old-school engineering. When Adrian came to us we weren't ready for him. When he went to McLaren and Williams they were very established teams. We didn't have the infrastructure they had. With Red Bull it was a clean piece of paper. A lot of people told him he was completely mad and he's proved them wrong. He has that element of flair and detail that pushes the boundaries.

He's great fun to be with and he's got a great sense of humour. Last winter we went to Graz in Austria, just before Christmas, to visit Dr Helmut Marko. Helmut is waiting for us at the end of this tree-lined drive. So Adrian decided to put in a power-slide and he understeered our car straight into one of the trees, taking the side out of the car. Just a typical Friday evening with Adrian Newey."

ALEX ALBON

(Red Bull)

"He was very connected to the driving side. He really wanted to know how it felt. His office was opposite Christian's, so I'd always go to see him. I was more involved with that kind of stuff speaking with Adrian during 2021, when I was more of a sim guy, trying to fix some of the issues we had in 2020, the same kind of things, understanding philosophies and what areas he needs to focus on.

If it was something that he felt was important, he'd always come and speak to me after a Sunday and want my opinion about it, which was nice to have that relationship with someone who's obviously so influential."

INDEX

PICTURE CREDITS

Thanks to Peter Nygaard at GrandPrixPhoto.com for supplying the photos with the following exceptions:

Alamy, pages 44, 194 (top), 206, 214
Aston Martin, pages 7, 191, 215
FIA, page 203
Getty Images, pages 33, 38, 39, 42 (bottom), 45, 46, 50, 53 (top), 59, 60, 70, 71, 73 (top), 78, 81, 89 (left), 97, 165, 178, 186, 194 (bottom), 202, 204, 211, 216, 218
GPCars4Sale.com, page 54
Red Bull, page 148, 187, 189, 212, 217, 220, 221, 222, 228, 229, 230, 236 (left)
Shenington Kart Racing Club, page 17
Sothebys, pages 26, 36, 39, 41
Tamiya, pages 14, 15
Wikimedia/Craig Howell, page 226

ALSO AVAILABLE FOR F1 FANS ...

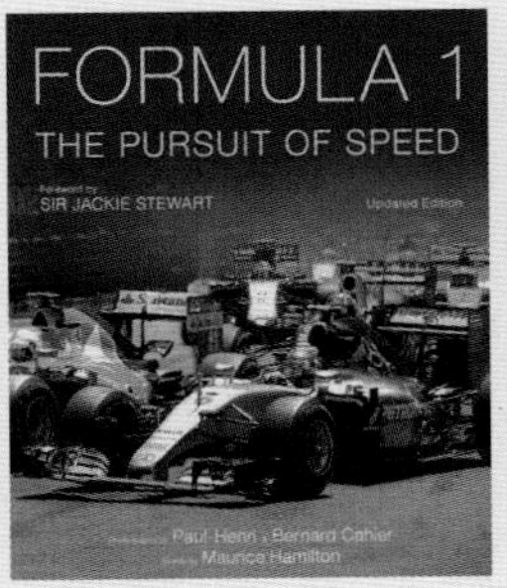

ISBN 9781781317082

ISBN 9780711274204

ISBN 9780711280717

ISBN 9780711289499

ISBN 9781836005650

ISBN 9780711298484

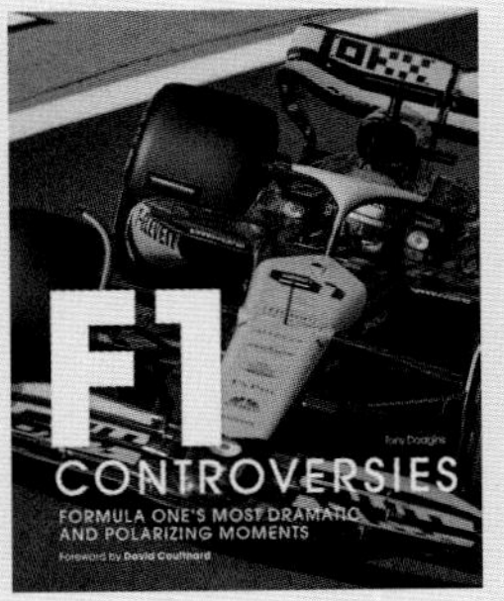

ISBN 9781805700296

ISBN 9781836005674